My Favourite Restaurants in Calgary & Banff

NEW EDITION

By

John Gilchrist
CBC Radio Restaurant Critic

Escurial Productions
Calgary Canada

Canadian Cataloguing in Publication Data

Gilchrist, John, 1953-
My favourite restaurants in Calgary & Banff

ISBN 0-9693106-1-7

1. Restaurants, lunch rooms, etc.—Alberta—Calgary—Guide-books.
2. Restaurants, lunch rooms, etc.—Alberta—Banff—Guide-books.
3. Calgary (Alta.)—Description—Guide-books.
4. Banff (Alta.)—Description—Guide-books.
I. Title. II. Title: My favourite restaurants in Calgary and Banff.
TX910.C2G54 1990   647.957123'3   C90-091653-2

Published by:
Escurial Productions
9519 - Assiniboine Road S.E.
Calgary, Alberta T2J 0Z5

Printed in Canada by:
Paperworks Press Limited
Calgary, Alberta

Cover Design by:
Michel Clairo
Out of the Blue Design Ltd.
Calgary, Alberta

Editing & Research by:
Cathy Caldwell

SECOND EDITION

ACKNOWLEDGEMENTS

Cathy Caldwell is the person most responsible for this book. Aside from her first-rate editing job, she's my wife and favourite dining partner. I also thank Bob Gerst — without his computer expertise we would still be rubbing two sticks together. Thanks also to my parents and to Cathy's for making not only us but this book possible. And I'm grateful to the good folks at the CBC for allowing me to air my views every Friday morning.

FOREWORD

Welcome to the second edition of *My Favourite Restaurants in Calgary & Banff*. Many changes have occurred in the restaurant industry since the first edition three years ago. Thai has arrived in full force, there's been a marked increase in other "ethnic" cuisines, and creatively contemporary restaurants are popping up all over. Humdrum Italian food is passé, Cajun is all but gone, and many restaurants have disappeared or moved or changed hands. So, it's time to pass on my new favourites.

You may notice that some of these are actually old favourites, places that appeared in the 1987 edition. I've revisited these establishments and written new reviews because they're still good. Others are completely new favourites, many of which have been adapted and updated from my weekly CBC Radio reviews. All together, this collection represents the cream of the culinary crop in the Calgary-Banff area — of the places I've visited that is. Even after ten years of restaurant reviewing, there are still many places that I've never been.

A note on reviewing: I don't reserve a table in my own name — that could lead to preferential treatment, and the review must be objective, based on the average customer's experience. So there goes that quiet little table in the corner by the fireplace. On the rare occasion that I may be recognized despite attempts to conceal my identity, I state this up front in my review. I also pay for my meals when I'm reviewing — no freebies.

A warning: I've updated each entry so that it's as current as possible. But restaurants frequently change — it may be the hours or the menu or the location or even the ownership. Keep this in mind when you're choosing a place to eat.

If credit cards are accepted, I've used the following abbreviations: **V-Visa; M-MasterCard; AE-American Express; ER-EnRoute; DC-Diners Club; JCB-Japan Credit Bureau**.

Cost ratings have been based on a dinner for two and include appetizers, main courses, and desserts (or the equivalent of this). Tips and alcohol haven't been included. **Cheap places cost less than $25, moderate $25 to $50, and expensive over $50**.

I hope you enjoy *My Favourite Restaurants*, both the food and the reviews. I'm going on a diet until the next edition.

CONTENTS

CARIBBEAN

ISLAND EXPERIENCE -
THE ROTI SHOP

314 - 10 Street N.W. 270-4550

Sun, noon - 9pm; Tues-Thurs, 11am - 9pm; Fri & Sat,
11am - 10pm. Reservations accepted. Beer & wine. No
non-smoking section. V, M, AE. Take-out. Cheap.

When was the last time you tasted a good goat dish? It's not available
in too many places, but it is, as an occasional special, at Island
Experience - The Roti Shop.

The Island Experience is a fast food kind of place, but it's not your
typical hamburger and sandwich joint. The menu features Caribbean
foods. It's an interesting collection, reflecting the East Indian and African
influences on the cuisine. On the Indian side, the roti is a large, circular
flat bread filled with a meat or vegetable curry and folded into a neat
little package. On the African side is the pelau, a mixture of cooked rice
and peas. Most of the dishes are heavy with rich Caribbean spices.

I've eaten there a few times, and recently, I had a puréed red lentil
soup with cassava dumplings. The soup was smooth and orange. The
dumplings were made from a mixture of cornmeal and flour from the
cassava root. I followed that with a goat roti, a big serving of stewed,
curried goat with potatoes and a spicy mango sauce. My whole plate was
very tasty. Not overly spicy, but filled with Caribbean flavour. The trouble
with goat meat is that, though it has great texture and a strong flavour, it
is very bony. And although the Island Experience prepares it well, they
still haven't gotten around this problem.

The only items actually cooked offsite are the Jamaican patties
(crescent-shaped pastry filled with spiced meat or vegetables) which
come from Lloyd's Caribbean Bakery in the Southeast. They prepare
everything else in an open kitchen no larger than the seating area, which
likely seats no more than twenty.

Of course the tropical drinks come from the islands. Some of these are
wonderful, like the mango or passion fruit, but watch out for the mauby,

a drink made from carob bark and aniseed. It is a syrupy, dark liquid that is definitely an aquired taste. It's kind of like a sour licorice drink. They do more than drinks and main courses though. MacKay's in Cochrane custom-makes their tropical ice cream with ingredients supplied by the Island Experience. It's good, packed with lots of fruit.

It's nice to sit in this bright, open café on a cold evening, sipping a glass of guava juice and enjoying a mango ice cream cone. It's a cozy little place with glass walls looking out onto 10th Street. It started out as an ice cream parlour, so it still retains that look. Some of the tables have high chairs, and all are small and round. It's a good thing meals aren't overly elaborate or they'd never fit on the tables.

The Island Experience has adjusted somewhat for Calgary palates and for the large number of vegetarian customers (most dishes are available without meat). And they don't do "Canadian" food at all. They do what they know, Caribbean food. And it makes for a nice lunch or quick dinner.

KIM'S DONAIR & JAMAICAN CUISINE

121 - 7 Avenue S.W. 263-3773

Sun, 2pm - 7:30pm; Mon-Fri, 9am - 10pm; Sat, 10:30am - 9:30pm. Reservations accepted. Unlicensed. Totally non-smoking. No credit cards. Take-out. Cheap.

After complaining about some jerk chicken on the radio one week, a friend called to tell me that if I really wanted some good stuff, I should get on over to Kim's Donair & Jamaican Cuisine. Not only do they make impressive jerk chicken, he told me, but they serve cows' feet too. So I figured, okay, I've had pigs' ears, bears' claws, and even ducks' feet — I better get down to Kim's and see what's up.

Kim's is hard to find, buried in behind the Centre Street LRT stop. It's a very tiny corner of a very dingy building. Not at all pretty. It's a short, narrow room with the kitchen up front and a window onto 7th Avenue for take-out. Past the kitchen are three rows of tables and chairs wobbling on pocked linoleum. A couple of tables have video-game tops, and a bulletin board announces Caribbean activities. It's not very pleasant, but it's not totally grungy either. It's just very spare and casual. But the smiles of the people working there warm it up.

Posted on various inconveniently placed boards are the house Jamaican specials — rotis, curries, patties, soursop drinks, and even the cow foot. To place your order, you almost have to shout over the hip-hop music blasting away.

I ordered a platter of curried lamb and jerk chicken. For $7, a huge plate was inundated with food. There was a big pile of rice laced with black beans that gave a smoky, almost chocolaty flavour. Beside it sat a pile of rather uncomplicated but spicy-hot cubed lamb and the jerk chicken. Squeezed into the corner of the plate was a mixed green salad. When I ordered the chicken I was told that it was very, very, very, very, very, very hot, which is a good guideline because now I know I can handle five "verys." That sixth one just about fried my face. Made with a sauce of West Indian Scotch bonnet peppers, it packed an incredible punch. But through the sauce, the chicken itself was well roasted and juicy. I honestly can't say if it was tasty since I couldn't find my way through the spice.

I also tried one of their patties, finely ground beef rolled into pastry — a touch oily, but still good. (Actually, it had been made at Lloyd's Caribbean Bakery.)

My biggest disappointment was the cow foot. They were out. A run on it that day, I suppose. But they assured me that this stewed delicacy was very good. My friend says that it is sort of gelatinous. Maybe next time.

Kim's biggest problem is the haphazard way they chop the meat. I found sharp shards of bone in both my lamb and my chicken. They don't seem too picky about the cuts of meat either, with seemingly everything going into the pot. And eating off styrofoam with plastic utensils is kind of food fare-ish, not to mention environmentally unsound. Regardless, it's good, basic Jamaican food. Where the Middle Eastern donair fits in, I'm not sure, but they do serve it.

LLOYD'S CARIBBEAN BAKERY

7, 3745 - Memorial Drive S.E. 248-2113

Mon-Fri, 8am - 7pm; Sat, 8am - 6pm. Unlicensed. No credit cards. Mainly take-out. Cheap.

I'd been bemoaning the fact that so many restaurants wouldn't commit themselves to fully using the spices and herbs available to them. Then I went to Lloyd's Caribbean Bakery. I bought some of Lloyd's jerk chicken to-go. It came with a hot sauce which Lloyd put in a separate container because, as he said with a knowing smile, "You might not like it."

I smirked a little. "The hot sauce that can do me in has not been invented," I thought.

So I went home with my chicken. I dipped a piece in the hot sauce. I popped it in my mouth, and I spent the next half-hour picking my eyeballs up off the floor. Lloyd doesn't hold back at all. That was the hottest sauce I have ever had, well beyond my control. I challenge anyone to find a hotter one in Calgary.

But don't let the sauce scare you. The jerk chicken itself, which is marinated overnight in pimento and other island spices, is dynamite. Grilled quickly, it has a soft black skin and is extremely moist. It's served in chunks like the duck in Chinatown. Great picnic food.

Lloyd whips up other Jamaican specialties in the back room. He makes very good curried goat and curried chicken. Done Jamaican-style, these are heavier on the chili peppers than their East Indian counterparts. His patties, half moons of flaky pastry filled with spiced beef hamburger, are a Jamaican tradition in the order of our hot dogs and are a popular item for only a buck a piece. He also makes vegetable, chicken, and shrimp patties for $1, $1.75, and $2 respectively. And he carries a Jamaican cheddar cheese that is reminiscent of Velveeta.

On the baked goods side, you can find lots of sturdy baking like the loaves of hard dough bread, a form of sourdough made with a lot of flour and little yeast. It's heavy and dense, silky smooth, and a little bit sweet. There are hard dough spice buns with fruit that would make an excellent alternative to hot cross buns at Easter. There's cornmeal bread, French bread, and ginger muffins.

Lloyd uses a lot of ginger. He makes his own ginger beer, which is almost too strong for me to consume. Although it's only ginger root, bitters, sugar, and water, it is a pungent brew that burns your mouth. I could only drink half my glass before I was overpowered. There are tropical fruit drinks like mango nectar which, oddly enough, come from Okokie, Illinois.

Lloyd's is a real gathering place for the Caribbean community. Lining the walls are flyers inviting anyone to parties and calypso nights at homes and community halls. There's a relaxed island feeling here, with reggae music and the lilt of Jamaican voices in the air. The five stools are filled with people who come from all over town for this food.

And then there's Lloyd himself, a smiling fellow who knows his customers and is generous with his free samples. He's had the bakery since 1984 and thinks he'll open a full-fledged restaurant someday. He's pretty sharp, and doesn't exactly give his food away: The hard dough bread is $2 a loaf; the jerk chicken, $8 a pound; and the cheese, also $8 a pound.

If you're just back from a Caribbean vacation or looking for the hottest sauce in town, pop into Lloyd's.

CHINESE

CHARLY CHAN'S RICE HOUSE

1140 - Kensington Road N.W. 283-6165

Peking & Szechwan. Sun-Thurs, 11am - 11pm; Fri & Sat,
11am - midnight. Reservations recommended for 6 or
more. Fully licensed. Non-smoking section. V, M, AE, ER.
Take-out. Summer outdoor dining. Moderate.

Our most recent visit to Charly Chan's was on a cool Sunday evening around 6 o'clock. I expected it to be, at most, half full. But it was packed! I realize that a few patrons were refuelling on their way to an Almodovar film at the Plaza, but many more were simply there for a casual early dinner.

We couldn't decide on appetizers so we started with Charly's combination platter of wontons, dry ribs, satay, and spring rolls. Often plates like this exude only one flavour, and this one did resemble one large brown lump. But the individual nibblies were, for the most part, dynamite. The wontons and spring rolls were packed with fresh herbs, the pork satays jumped in a deep-flavoured peanut sauce, and the ribs — well, what can I say? They were ribs. Deep-fried ribs. Ribs never seem to have enough meat on them for me, but what was on these bones was tender enough.

Our indecision carried through into the main courses, so we ordered far too much for two people — sizzling shrimp, Mandarin chicken, and spicy beef. And on the recommendation of our waitress, we tried two rolls (one steamed, one deep-fried) instead of rice. These are submarine-shaped loaves of bread made with rice flour and kneaded with arm-stretching, toffee-pulling movements until the interior of each loaf looks like strands of noodles packed together. They're perfect for soaking up sauces from your other dishes.

And good sauces these are too. Both our sizzling shrimp and spicy beef came in chili-laden, hoisin-based ones. Dark and spicy, they coated the crunchy shrimp and lean beef like a glove. The Mandarin chicken was more sweet than sour, so we were happy that we had ordered it extra hot. The chilies helped cut through some of the sweetness.

All this lightened the old credit card by $45, not the cheapest meal in town, but we felt we had received more than adequate compensation. And we rolled home with mega-leftovers.

Charly Chan's has one of Calgary's shortest Chinese menus — forty-two items, including desserts. But it's supplemented by a number of daily specials like our spicy beef.

I don't know why, but I'm always amazed at how good Chan's is. I suppose it's because, with a name like Charly Chan's, I almost expect a North American version of Chinese food. But that's not what you get. It's straight ahead Peking and Szechwan fare that cuts no corners.

DRAGON PEARL

1223A - 9 Avenue S.E. 233-8810

Peking & Szechwan. Sun, 5pm - 9:30pm; Mon-Thurs, 5pm - 10:30pm; Fri & Sat, 5pm - 11pm; Sun-Sat, 11am - 2pm. Reservations accepted. Beer & wine. Non-smoking section. V, M, AE. Take-out. Sat & Sun dim sum. Moderate.

In any city there are a few dining treasures buried somewhere on the industrial back streets. Often surrounded by businesses of questionable natures, hiding behind dirty windows, one can find the most delightful diners. Such is the case with the Dragon Pearl, a favourite of mine for years. I'm speaking about the 9th Avenue location near the Zoo turnoff on 12th Street S.E., not the new, yuppified Westbrook Mall location.

The old Dragon Pearl used to have the tackiest decor imaginable — gold-flaked mirrors crashed into red velvet wallpaper on one side and metallic bronze wallpaper on the other. Real nice. Attempts at gentrification (including bowls without chips) have subdued it somewhat, but it's still a long, narrow room with the bathrooms down a precarious staircase.

Their extensive menu is augmented by daily specials. One I tried lately was a plate of lemon shrimp, a tangy concoction with what seemed like half a grocery bag of huge crustaceans. Another special that day was beef and snow peas in black bean sauce. It took advantage of seasonal peas and onions, and a bunch of whole black beans supplemented the rich, spicy sauce. Yet another daily special was the salt and pepper ribs in a thin batter. Nice flavour. We rounded out our meal with one item off the regular menu, the jumpingly spicy ginger-fried chicken.

The Dragon Pearl has gone quietly about its business over the years, keeping up with the Szechwan and Peking food trends. I find their food to be consistently fresh, well prepared, and interesting. It's served in huge quantities too. They never seem to compromise. If you want middle-of-the-road fare, there are lots of other places to eat. But people want to eat here. I've seen customers lined up down the street. And aside from the food, service has always been friendly and pleasant.

A second location opened in October of 1988 in Westbrook Mall at 1002B - 37 Street S.W. (246-2253).

GOLDEN FORTUNE

106, 111 - 3 Avenue S.E. 269-8388

Cantonese & Peking. Sun, 10am - 2am; Mon-Thurs, 10:30am - 2am; Fri & Sat, 10am - 3am. Reservations recommended on weekends. Fully licensed. Non-smoking section. V, M, AE, DC. Take-out. Karaoke. Cheap-moderate.

I had been suffering through some serious dental work, and my appetite was leaning away from corn-on-the-cob and peanut brittle. I was much more interested in custards and cream cheese and soft Oriental noodles, so I visited one of Chinatown's new wave of eateries, the Golden Fortune Restaurant. It falls into the category that is loosely referred to as noodle houses, places that serve a whole meal in a little bowl for a little price. At least, this is largely what the Golden Fortune does at lunchtime. They go beyond the noodle house mode by offering a full menu of Cantonese and Peking food in the evening.

The Golden Fortune is on the lower level of the Good Fortune Plaza, a newish building in the heart of Chinatown. It fits the look of a typical noodle house. It's square and homely with too many mirrors and fluorescent lights that bounce off the arborite, making everyone look half dead. The purple carpet has seen too much traffic, the huge collection of crockery is cracked, and they use every possible inch for eating space. There's even a small table stuffed into a corner with two chairs facing the mirrored wall. Great for watching yourself eat, unless you don't like the fluorescent pallor.

But ambience is not the selling point of a noodle house. What does sell is the fact that you can get in, be seated, order, eat, and leave in under twenty minutes. Fifteen if you're in a hurry. If a leisurely lunch is more to your liking and you don't mind the bodies flying past, the tea never stops. The minute you sit down, a steaming pot arrives at your table, and if you manage to finish it, it's whisked off for a refill. Your order is taken as quickly as you can decide, and the food is delivered as fast as it can be assembled (most things are pre-prepared at lunch).

Most lunch dishes are bowls of broth filled with rice or noodles. Toppings include various vegetables and meats in sauces, like roast pork in hot sauce or preserved Chinese radish with shredded duck. I've tried an excellent combination of barbecued pork, roast pork, chicken, and barbecued duck on soft noodles. With about four ounces of each meat, a huge pile of noodles in a bowl of broth, and a pot of tea, it's hard to believe that I only paid $4.95. But perhaps the best deal is their rice rolls. These are slimy, white, rice pancakes filled with meat. You can get three big ones filled with pork or beef or chicken for only $1.75. For shrimp rolls (and they use a lot of very good shrimp), the price jumps to an amazing $1.95.

The Golden Fortune is less frantic than the Hang Fung next door, and not quite as packed as the Double Greeting down the street. Staff are excellent — helpful and friendly. And where else can you get a cup of Ovaltine these days?

HANG FUNG

119 - 3 Avenue S.E. 269-5853

Cantonese & Peking. Sun-Thurs, 9am - 9pm; Fri & Sat, 9am - 10pm. Reservations accepted for dinner. Unlicensed. No non-smoking section. No credit cards. Cheap.

Chinatown is always a buzz of activity. One of the busiest and most popular spots is the Hang Fung Restaurant. If you haven't heard of it, don't be surprised. It's hard to find, and even people who have eaten there aren't sure what it's called.

It's often referred to as the little noodle house beside the Ruby Restaurant, and it's hidden behind the Hang Fung Grocery, a fruit and vegetable shop on 3rd Avenue. Once you've made your way through the greenery, around the corner to the left, and through a door, you'll find the restaurant — a long narrow room that seats about fifty. It's usually quite full, so the lack of signs doesn't seem to have hurt them.

The crowds aren't coming for the decor. The Hang Fung is not one of Chinatown's more elegant restaurants. It's of the fluorescent mode. Every square inch of space has a purpose. If there are empty seats at your table, chances are that a few strangers will be plunked there. Singles are seated at the counter where they'll have no place to tuck their knees if they are unlucky enough to be put at one end.

This is fast food Chinese-style. There is no time for formality or modesty. It's a refuelling station. Take a seat, order now, slurp it down, and get out. But you *can* take as long as you want. It's just that you might not *want* to take a long time. Maybe twenty, twenty five minutes. That's about all you'll need. Service follows the swiftness of preparation. The staff can be friendly, but mostly they're efficient.

They specialize in one plate meals — a big pile of rice or noodles topped with meats or vegetables. Things like beef in black bean sauce on fried noodles or barbecued duck on rice, both about $4. They also do rice pancakes, rolled and filled with shrimp or pork or green onion for less than two bucks. The dumplings, which are grilled in seconds, are among the freshest and tastiest in town.

A favourite of mine is the barbecued pork lo-mein. A platter is filled with vermicelli noodles that have been lightly fried. It seems like half a pound of boneless barbecued pork is dumped on top. It's a huge serving for the $4.25 price. But beware. Even the best Chinese barbecue chefs can sometimes overdo the meat, leaving it dry. Nevertheless, the taste is always incredible.

Some dishes loose out under the demands of quick preparation. For instance, an oyster and roast pork hot pot came out with too much oyster sauce, destroying any balance with the pork.

But all in all, a quick plate of pretty decent food for real cheap. That's the theme of the Hang Fung. Don't forget your wallet though. They only take cash.

HOME FOOD INN

4714 - 1 Street S.W. 243-1610

Peking. Sun-Thurs, 5pm - 9:30pm; Fri & Sat, 5pm - 10:30pm; Mon-Fri, 11am - 2pm. Reservations recommended for 5 or more. Fully licensed. Non-smoking section. V, M, AE. Take-out. Moderate.

You find the best restaurants in the darndest places. Squeezed in between some body shops off Macleod Trail is the Home Food Inn, where it has been since 1982. Someone seems to have realized the shortcomings of its location because they've clad the exterior in bright blue, red, and orange. It practically glows in the dark now.

Faithful followers of fine food being what they are, it is often full. That's because it's a pleasant place that produces a crisply fresh rendition of Peking cuisine — spicy hot if you want, mild if you prefer.

Over one-hundred items are listed on the menu, running the gamut from shellfish and poultry to bean curd and veggies to noodles and dumplings. With such variety, you can get quite adventurous. How about braised oysters with ginger and spring onions or bean curd with minced pork in a chili sauce? Then there's always sweet-and-sour pork or shrimp-fried rice. If you like the old standards, they do chicken and cashews in yellow bean sauce and deep-fried shredded beef with chilies (the ubiquitous ginger beef) as well as anyone else. The flavours at the Home Food Inn jump out, making each dish as interesting as the first time you tasted it.

It hasn't really changed much over the years, even though it's under new ownership. The menu is the same, the chef is the same, the food is pretty much the same. There's lots of tea, piles of steamed rice, and a smiling staff. And a good deal on mufflers just down the street.

KAM HAN

Macleod Trail & Lake Fraser Gate S.E.
(Avenida Bonavista Shopping Centre) 278-1211

*Peking & Szechwan. Sun & holidays, 4pm - 10:30pm;
Mon-Thurs, 5pm - 10:30pm; Fri & Sat, 4:30pm -
11:30pm; Mon-Fri, 11am - 2pm. Reservations
recommended, especially on weekends. Fully licensed.
Non-smoking section. V, M, AE. Take-out. Moderate.*

Szechwan food moved into prominence quickly a few years ago,
drawing fans of Peking who wanted more strength and complexity in
their mouths and some just plain different stuff. Attesting to this is the
fact that Kam Han Szechwan House opened a second location. Their first
is behind the Stampede grounds on Spiller Road, and now they're in
Avenida Bonavista, a pretty shopping mall that only seems to be busy at
its north end where all the restaurants are.

Avenida's Kam Han is a large room, utilitarian yet pretty in turquoise.
The tables and bamboo chairs can be quickly shifted about to
accommodate groups. And their Szechwan-style of food, combined with
this casual atmosphere, does seem to attract groups. While we were
there, one batch of fifteen was balanced off by a party of nine.

The menu includes some Peking dishes too, like chicken and cashews
and the famous Peking duck, as well as a few dishes from Mongolia and
the province of Hunan. We tried some thinly sliced Mongolian beef in a
light green curry with green onions and bell peppers. Lean and tender, the
meat let off a little bite, but nothing excessive. Our pork tenderloin with
black peppercorn sauce was cooked in another rich, garlicky sauce, this
one more peppery. A good dish, but the quality of pork led me to believe
that it may not have been all tenderloin. Pork tenderloin is one of my
favourite meats to both cook and eat, and I've never seen any with that
much fat. Our third main dish was salt and pepper chicken. Kam Han's
version comes in an unfortunately thick batter, leaving a Colonel Sanders
impression. It tastes fine, but I'd like more chicken and less batter.

One thing I really like at Kam Han is their grilled dumplings. It seems
that these half-moons have become a real marker of northern Chinese
food. There are those who live only for the quintessential dumpling. The
Kam Han's are big, without too much dough. The minced pork and
vegetables are juicy and full of flavour. The dough is just the right
consistency, balanced between crunchy and chewy. Very hard to fault.
And if you're a non-purist dumpling eater, there's a bowl of hot sauce
and bottles of soy sauce or vinegar for dunking.

You'll also find lemon shrimp, fried noodles, and the ever-popular
ginger-fried beef to go along with Szechwan bean curd and curried beef
soup with vermicelli. It's a good menu, reasonably priced, and pretty
well prepared.

So, although I wouldn't rank Kam Han at the top of the Szechwan-

Peking heap, it does sit up there with the second bests. First spot is reserved for Leo Fu's until further notice.

Kam Han's first location is at 2016 - Spiller Road S.E. (264-6030).

LAKE SYLVAN PALACE

12, 1215 - Lake Sylvan Drive S.E. 271-9366

Peking. Sun & holidays, 4:30pm - 9:30pm; Mon & Tues, 4:30pm - 10:30pm; Wed & Thurs, 4:30pm - 11pm; Fri & Sat, 4:30pm - midnight. Reservations recommended. Fully licensed. No non-smoking section. V, M, AE. Take-out. Moderate.

Lake Sylvan Palace is nowhere near Sylvan Lake. It's buried in the depths of Lake Bonavista on Lake Sylvan Drive, hence the name. Tucked into a homely strip mall, the kind with ugly post-modern peaks stuck on the outside, the unwelcoming exterior hides a pretty restaurant of pink and grey and black. None of the fluorescent lights, red vinyl, and peeling linoleum of ancient chop suey houses. The pink linen napkins, grey carpet, and offset lighting confer a little softness, a little elegance.

The stylish look carries over into the food. Although the menu doesn't vary significantly from most Peking restaurants, they have a knack for being just a little bit better. Maybe it's higher quality ingredients or their modern kitchen, or maybe it's just a cook with a deft hand.

My first experience with Lake Sylvan Palace was during a Chinese New Year celebration. I was impressed with their twelve-course meal. Everything was top quality, presented with a flare, and dished out in healthy portions. But ever the cynic, I wondered if they would be as good when there wasn't a special event. So I've been back a couple of times and found that, if anything, they are better.

One highlight is their salt and pepper shrimp. Lightly battered and quick-fried with a bite of pepper, it's a great way to prepare shrimp and other seafood. This is the dish that is supplanting ginger beef as the next Chinese food obsession. Oh, they still have the ginger beefs and the pineapple chicken balls, but their versions seem to hold less oil and more flavour than most.

The chicken and cashews are done well. Not over-loaded with celery but nicely balanced with large chunks of chicken and loads of cashews in a rich, dark bean sauce. The grilled pork dumplings are crisp on the outside, smooth on the inside. There's beef or shrimp, pungent in heavy green curries. There's a Szechwan-style, spicy eggplant dish. There's sizzling rice and hot pots and fried noodles.

The wine list is short and sweet — a good attribute for some things, though not for wine. But then, there's lots of beer and tea, and those go better with Chinese food anyway.

Service is friendly and quick. The two guys who own and run Lake Sylvan Palace are young and ambitious and trying hard to please. And they are doing a fine job.

LEO FU'S

511 - 70 Avenue S.W. 255-2528

Szechwan & Mandarin. Sun-Thurs, 5pm - 10pm; Fri & Sat, 5pm - midnight; Mon-Fri, 11:30am - 2pm. Reservations accepted. Fully licensed. Non-smoking section. V, M, AE. Take-out. Moderate.

What more can I say about the best Szechwan restaurant in Calgary? Ever since my first visit to Leo Fu's, I have been a tub-thumping fan. And I'm certainly not alone in my opinion. Regulars are almost religious in their admiration. Yet many people don't know of Leo Fu's because of its obscure location off Macleod Trail. Others have told me it's just too far away. Well, Leo Fu's is definitely worth the trip.

Once you've made it to Leo Fu's, you'll likely be greeted by one of the Koo family, the people who own and operate the place. (Not one of them is named Leo — Leo Fu actually translates as lucky six.) You'll be seated in a bright rectangular room on a carved rosewood chair at a table draped in blue. If you have twenty or thirty friends to bring along, you can reserve the private room at the back. Once seated, you'll be handed a menu that is far more extensive than most others of the Peking/Szechwan/Mandarin vein.

Decisions can be tough, so here are a few suggestions. I love their orange-flavoured beef with its big chunks of crunchy, tender meat laminated in a pungent orange sauce. Then there's the boneless and spicy General Tso's chicken. The "double delicacy" is a smooth combination of chicken and pork, each in its own sauce. The Shang-Hai duck mixes broccoli, snow peas, and raisins with the fowl in a sweet and salty Mandarin sauce. Hunan beef, Szechwan eggplant, fragrant crispy duck, salt and pepper squid, double-cooked pork — the list goes on and on and always changes a bit too.

It's the sauces that really make Leo Fu's exceptional. Thick and savoury and not particularly spicy-hot, they are strong, forceful concoctions. They don't use MSG — it may be present in some of the pre-prepared sauces, but they don't add any additional stuff. It's rich food that's not for the meek. Leo Fu's is also one of the few Chinese restaurants where the ingredients aren't chopped into teeny scraps. You get food that you can actually pick up with chopsticks, and if you get really big chunks, the pieces are usually tender enough to bite through. Most other places wouldn't dare risk such bulk.

Service at Leo Fu's is always elegant and punctual. Food presentation is superb, with some dishes almost too pretty and colourful to eat. As long as Leo Fu's continues to choose interesting dishes, prepare them with top-quality ingredients, and serve them with such panache, they will continue to be Number One. The only place closing in on them is their new take-out location in Shawnessy (627 - Shawcliffe Gate S.W., 254-1688). Take-out is also available at the original place.

SHAN TUNG

332 - 14 Street N.W. 283-3388

Peking & Szechwan. Sun, 4:30pm - 10pm; Mon-Thurs, 4:30pm - 11pm; Fri & Sat, 4:30pm - midnight; Mon-Fri, 11am - 2pm. Reservations recommended on weekends. Fully licensed. Non-smoking section. V, M, AE. Take-out. Cheap-moderate.

A few winters ago I drove up Crowchild Trail every Saturday morning on my way to a French class at the university. As the widening of Crowchild and my knowledge of French both progressed, various buildings began to disappear. To my chagrin, so did the scuzzy little mall right on the corner of Crowchild and Kensington Road. Not that it was an architectural landmark. In fact, it was quite ugly. But it did house one of our best Peking and Szechwan restaurants. The Shan Tung was a homely little place, with glaring fluorescents and bumpy linoleum. Its claim to fame was good, cheap food in huge quantities.

Fortunately for Shan Tung fans, the restaurant only moved, and not too far away either. It's a much newer building that, in spite of its youth, is as ugly as its predecessor. On the outside, a busy mess of brick and wood make it almost impossible to find the door. Inside, it exudes the stylish look of Chinese restaurants of my youth — lots of black, uncomfortable red velveteen booths, arborite tables, and a fish tank. Concessions for the '90s include separate rooms for smoking and fresh air and a colour TV to watch the Stamps beat the Lions.

So decor is still not the Shan Tung's strong suit. First and foremost, it continues to be the food. They were one of the first to offer Peking and Szechwan fare, and they've kept up with the industry instead of getting locked into a ginger-beef mentality. They offer a lot of dishes that aren't seen in too many places, like shredded duck soup or spinach noodles with vegetables, as well as the old standbys like chicken and cashews in yellow bean sauce. You can mix a meal of standards with newcomers.

One of the appetizers is a dish that's currently popular, salt and pepper seafood. Scallops, prawns, and squid are deep-fried in a batter laced with salt and pepper and, in this recipe, hot chilies as well. Theirs is a good version because the batter is crisp and not too thick, and the seafood is juicy and hot.

Their hot-and-sour-soup on sizzling rice provides an Eastern style of the old snap, crackle, pop. Rice cakes, still hot from deep-frying, are doused with soup at your table to produce a real sizzle. The crispy rice adds another texture to an already very good soup filled with pork, tofu, vegetables, and mushrooms.

The mui-she pork is a dish of stir-fried pork, vegetables, and egg that you roll inside wheat pancakes after adding a disturbingly pink sauce. I'd like it better if this sauce wasn't so sweet (or so pink). And I always wonder why they only give you four pancakes when there's enough mui-she for twelve. Oh well.

The hot plate of fried noodles with black pepper and shredded beef is worth ordering. It's light and fresh and very *nouvelle Chinoise*, yet has a bite that builds slowly but undeniably from its load of black pepper.

There are over one-hundred items on the menu. Most are in the $7 to $9 range, with most seafood under $10. And they don't skimp — I'm a serious pig, and sometimes I can hardly make a dent. Another thing that has carried over from the old Shan Tung is the service. They are very attentive, constantly refilling water glasses and tea pots and checking to ensure that your food is satisfactory.

So in spite of the move, or perhaps because of it, the Shan Tung is as good as ever. Maybe even better.

SILVER INN

2702 - Centre Street N. 276-6711

Peking. Sun, Tues-Thurs, 5pm - 11pm; Fri & Sat, 5pm - midnight; Tues-Fri, 11am - 2pm. Reservations accepted. Fully licensed. Non-smoking section. V, M. Take-out. Moderate.

A decade and a half ago I sampled my first Peking dumpling, my first ginger beef, and my first chicken and cashews in yellow bean sauce at a grotty little place on 4th Street S.W. Long before that strip became trendy, the Silver Inn initiated a lot of people to the then unknown intricacies of Peking cuisine. It was a dive of a place with potholes in the linoleum that were big enough to lose your VW beetle in. There was just enough grunge in the corners to make me feel that I was going against every food rule my mother taught me.

A lot of years have passed since then, and the Silver Inn moved to Centre Street quite a while ago. Occasionally I, like many other Peking food fans, trek over to this shrine of Eastern cuisine that's always packed. Their menu is a lot the same. Oh, they've included more current dishes, but the old faves remain — it seems like every second dish wheeled out of the kitchen is either ginger beef or grilled dumplings.

A small group of us tucked into a fair-sized meal there recently. Beef and broccoli, salt and pepper pork, spicy chicken balls, scallops in black bean sauce, dumplings, and onion pancakes. Some dishes were very good — the pancakes and the beef and broccoli in particular. And their dumplings still define the word for me. But the chicken and pork dishes were pointless — no flavour, no snap, just balls of deep-fried goo that sat in my stomach for hours. And the scallops hadn't been adequately cleaned — we kept biting down on sand.

The funny thing is, I almost didn't notice these faux pas. I'd come to think of the Silver Inn as a classic, timeless, unchanging place, and I was caught up in memories of good times and great tastes. But a neophyte diner, not familiar with the history, suggested to me mid-meal that some of this food was not particularly good. I had to admit, on reflection and with more attention to my taste buds, that she was right. I was tasting my memories rather than the food.

This of course made me wonder, "Was it ever that good? Was I just thrilled by the newness of it back then? Or had it gone downhill? Had the Peking restaurants that followed now surpassed the originator?" I don't know the answers.

I'd like to think of the Silver Inn as one of the best, but right now, they've come back to the pack. Perhaps they were just having a bad night — we *did* have some decent dishes after all. On another night they might be back at the top. But maybe things just aren't the same anymore.

CONTEMPORARY

CILANTRO

338 - 17 Avenue S.W. 229-1177

Sun-Thurs, 11am - 11pm; Fri & Sat, 11am - midnight.
Reservations recommended. Fully licensed. Non-smoking
section. V, M, AE, DC. Summer outdoor dining. Sat & Sun
à la carte brunch. Moderate.

There are very few truly creative chefs in town, the kind who break away from the norm to create new dishes, the kind who look at food and figure out interesting things to do with it. One of the few is Dany Lamote, a culinary consultant who supervises the kitchens at Divino and that other hotbed of trendoidism, Cilantro.

Lamote has created a Southwestern-California menu based on items coming out of California, Arizona, New Mexico, and Mexico — pastas like jalapeno penne; soups like a crab, corn, and cactus chowder; sandwiches like chicken with capocollo, tomato, and pesto. There's an Eastern edge with rack of lamb in Hunan sauce, fresh mussels in black bean sauce, and fettuccine with pheasant and shiitake mushrooms in a ginger and wasabi sauce. They use a lot of fresh herbs, including their namesake, cilantro.

Cilantro the café took over what used to be Marty's, a smelly place that had great music and lousy food. Cilantro is nothing like Marty's. Cilantro was "Designed." They keyed in on the character of the buildings, one originally a tailor shop, the other a house. The front room is all wood and off-white. Facing south, full-length glass windows create a bright, almost deserty feel that goes along with the cuisine. The art deco salt and pepper shakers, the translucent lamp shades, and the oversized dinner plates add to the overall look. The attached building in the back houses Calgary's first wood-burning oven, and it produces innovative, thin-crusted pizzas topped with things like asiago cheese and pheasant.

Cilantro cries out for The Beautiful People — a clientele that will pose, that will look like they fell out of *Vogue* or a Woody Allen movie. And they get it. Regulars spend time preparing to see and be seen. They look just right in leather suits, rakish hats, carefully rumpled t-shirts, and

$60 haircuts. Cilantro diners are as deliberate as Cilantro's design.

But past the style and flash, Cilantro delivers surprisingly deep content. The food is beyond good. It is very fine, creative, and of course, pretty. I've had grilled swordfish that was stunning in its simplicity, spiked with a fruit chutney and a mustard-mint sauce. I've had a chicken sandwich with poultry as tender as I've ever tasted. I've had a corn and lettuce salad with so many herbs that my taste buds almost gave up in confusion. And I've had a quesadilla better than I've ever had in a Mexican restaurant. I've even had a hamburger with pancetta ham and Monterey jack cheese that was excellent. Their bread and buns and even their corn and cheddar cheese muffins are exceptional, all baked on the premises. Their desserts are among Calgary's finest. The food is very hard to fault.

If Cilantro has a drawback, it is in the service, which varies from reasonable to a very studied indifference. It can be frustratingly slow, but it seems there are few customers concerned with a sixty-minute lunch. Their other shortcoming is the air quality in the evenings. It is one of the few places where smoking a cigarette is still considered somewhat of an art form. And there is no particularly good provision for non-smokers.

Regardless, Cilantro has first-rate food. And a real trendy crowd. So don't leave home without the latest fashions.

DIVINO CAFE GALLERY

817 - 1 Street S.W. 263-5869

Mon-Thurs, 11am - 11pm; Fri & Sat, 11am - midnight.
Reservations accepted for large groups. Beer, wine &
liqueurs. Non-smoking section. V, M, AE, DC. Summer
outdoor dining. Moderate.

A lot of people did double takes when they saw Divino Cafe Gallery. The narrow little restaurant in the Grain Exchange Building had finally been accepted as the Cascade Grill after being dubbed Divino for the first few years of its life. Yes, that big hit of the early '80s, Divino, has resurfaced.

It looks a lot the same. They've done a few renovations with new paint and light fixtures, and they display art in conjunction with Paul Kuhn Fine Arts. But the original, decades-old style of the place still overpowers any details applied on it. Once upon a time a tailor shop, it has a deeply indented doorway, creating two tiny dining areas that used to be display windows. A tight corridor leads to a small space at the back. With waist-high wood panelling, high ceilings, a checkerboard floor, and a huge skylight, Divino has a distinctive, semi-bohemian look that sits well with its similar-looking clientele. The outdoor café almost doubles the seating during the summer, but it intrudes into a parking lot. Oh well. It costs to be trendy.

They call their food California-Italian. Dany Lamote puts the menu together here as well as that other high-tone spot, Cilantro. His focus is on unusual combinations of foods, seasonal ingredients, lots of herbs, and natural sauces that break from traditional techniques. Things like chicken breast stuffed with blueberries and mascarpone cheese. Such a flavour. Or jalapeno rotini with capocollo and green onions in a garlic and black bean sauce. Wonderful. There's so much culinary crossover with ingredients like black beans, tortillas, pesto, havarti, jalapenos, and even back bacon. Where else could you get panzarotti and fontina cheese on the same plate with salsa fresca and guacamole? Raised in Zaire and inspired by its food, Lamote created his black pepper linguine with chicken, tomatoes, spinach, and sesame seeds, an old but pleasant standby for Divino regulars. Recently I tried an excellent tomato and basil soup served with simple parmesan bread sticks made from their own bread which had been toasted with cheese and herbs.

In spite of all this innovation, they make one heck of a good burger, and prices are not outrageous. All dishes, like at Cilantro, appear with a simple dollar figure beside them — no cents tagged on here. With the priciest item at $11, it's always good value. They also brew one of the best cups of coffee in town and are one of the few restaurants to serve café au lait by the bowl.

Divino suffered from poor and/or slow service in the past. An efficient business lunch could stretch into an irritating hour and a half. But they seem to have become much quicker. And friendlier. Maybe they realized that even bohemian business people only have an hour for lunch and that they too like to smile.

THE DOCK

1600 - 90 Avenue S.W. (Glenmore Landing) 253-2542

Sun, 4pm - 9pm; Mon-Sat, 11:30am - 10pm. Reservations recommended. Fully licensed. Non-smoking section. V, M, AE. Summer outdoor dining. Moderate-expensive.

For the first few years after Glenmore Landing opened, it lacked an eatery to match the overall tone of the place. But now there is The Dock, a place that not only fits the upscale look, but fills a huge niche for fresh seafood aficionados.

The spot used to be an ice cream parlour. At first glance, moored next to the Pizza Bank and a McDonald's, The Dock looks like just another fish and chips shop. But behind those white venetian blinds they are serving superb seafood with light, interesting sauces at good prices. And there's not a deep-fried shrimp on the menu.

It has been thoroughly renovated from its ice cream days. It's done in a '90s, grey and white theme with lots of windows and a high ceiling where a canoe and a fishing dory hang. The clean lines are warmed by a barrage of plants and a green ceramic-tile floor. Grey vinyl coverings and sparse white dishes top the tables, along with small salt and pepper grinders — a thoughtful touch that I wish more restaurants would include.

The menu dispels any last thoughts of fish and chips. There's grilled salmon and halibut, shrimp cocktail, oysters on the half-shell — all solid, traditional seafood dishes. Then there are vodka prawns, scallop crêpes with lobster sauce, cognac-marinated salmon, and calamari with wild mushrooms. The Dock really hits its stride with daily specials like stuffed green mussels or orange roughy in blueberry sauce. Make sure your server tells you about the specials. Sometimes they forget, and the board that lists them is not readable from certain seating areas.

We both started with a salmon chowder — a buttery, milky bath filled with pieces of potato with the skin still on, bits of onion, and big chunks of salmon. It wasn't the least bit overcooked or falsely thickened with flour or cornstarch, two common faults of chowders.

I ordered the balance of my meal from the appetizer side of the menu — first the cognac-marinated salmon, then the calamari with wild mushrooms. The salmon was served gravlax-style with four thick, dill-covered slices on a bed of lettuce with a big dollop of mustard-dill mayonnaise. Just terrific. It's not for everyone since this preparation is much rawer and fleshier than smoked salmon, but it blends the delicate flavours perfectly. I ordered the calamari last due to the spiciness of the sauce. A thin, herbed tomato sauce with tons of calamari and mushrooms, it was a good dish. The squid may have been cooked a little too long or a little too hot because it was a bit chewy. Not anywhere near the pink eraser stage though.

My partner followed her chowder with orange roughy in an orange sauce. A short, fat fish, orange roughy cooks wonderfully with light sauces. This one was sautéed to perfection. Delicately orange-flavoured, the fillets were served with zucchini, new potatoes, and pieces of fruit. As a daily special with the chowder, the price-tag was only $9.75.

Just when we thought it was safe to leave the table, the dessert menu arrived. We never had a chance. A hefty carrot cake snagged my companion. A three chocolate mousse combo — white, dark, and milk — with a raspberry purée lured me. Deadly. Except I got two lumps of milk chocolate mousse and no dark. I'd have been real ornery if it had been the other way around since I'm a milk chocolate fan.

I have only two other concerns with The Dock. When they first opened, they served the most wonderful dinner rolls. The last time I ate there, these had been replaced with quite ordinary ones. The other problem is accessibility for the handicapped. The washrooms are up a long flight of stairs, and with the overall tight setup of the restaurant, it looks like a difficult place to negotiate. But this is not totally The Dock's fault. Other parts of Glenmore Landing were built with access problems as well.

Anyway, food-wise and service-wise, The Dock is a winner. As long as they keep up their initial quality, they will do well.

GREEN STREET CAFÉ

815 - 7 Avenue S.W. 266-1551

Sun buffet brunch; Mon-Sat, open for dinner; Mon-Fri, open for lunch. Reservations recommended. Fully licensed. Non-smoking section. V, M, AE, ER, DC, JCB. Lounge. Summer outdoor dining. Moderate-expensive.

A lot of people swear by Green Street Café. I even have friends in Camrose who trek to Calgary just to eat there. When I reviewed it a couple of years ago, it was going through some uneven times in the kitchen, and I unfortunately hit it on a low swing. But my last few visits have swung pretty high.

Green Street has one of the best, if not *the* best, Sunday buffet brunches going. For a very reasonable $11.50, it's quite possible to do damage to yourself. A chef will prepare an omelette for you right then and there. I'm fond of their eggs Benedict, not an easy dish for a buffet line. Lots of fresh, good quality food instead of that greasy and cold stuff you see all over the place. A cautionary note: the staff may seem unprepared for early arrivals — sometimes they need coffee more than the customers.

Brunch aside, Green Street is popular with Calgary's Power Lunchers. It looks the part too. The floors and chairs are a calm but strong green. The crisp napkins and white china add a corporate sharpness. A panoramic view of a small park provides a pastoral hint, but the marble table-tops remind us that the hard edges aren't too far away. Wrapped around the base of the Nova Building downtown at 7th and 7th, a natty crowd of young movers and shakers blows off steam from morning meetings over lengthy meals. Conversations buzz about corporate memos and office politics while file folders and briefcases snap, crackle, and pop.

Sometimes *eating* lunch here seems secondary to *doing* lunch here, which is unfortunate because the food isn't bad. The mid-day menu is cute and quick and eclectic — Louisiana Creole soup, camembert and pear fritters with red currant sauce, Szechwan chicken, and beef kabobs. There's a handful of pastas and salads and a nod to the meat-and-potato crowd with a steak sandwich. Interesting preparation and presentation are the key, with some subtle flavours and some spicy ones. It's a menu that covers all the bases.

I delved into a lunch special that started with a cream of chicken soup with cheddar cheese. Velvetty smooth and loaded with delicate flavours, it was served with hot rolls baked on the premises. This could have stood as lunch in itself. Next came a beef bourguignon suffering the fate of those made with lesser qualities of meat. This one, although in a savoury sauce, demanded a strong, well-developed jaw. It arrived with a pile of rice, some red cabbage with raisins, and cheese-covered broccoli. A good looking plate with nice variety. I had my stomach set on the warm pecan tarts with banana ice cream for dessert, but since I wasn't power lunching, time did not permit.

Green Street takes on a whole different atmosphere for dinner — very calm and subdued. The menu expands a bit to items like orange roughy in a champagne sauce or rack of lamb with a dijon-maple syrup glaze, a potentially good dish that had been overdone for my taste when I tried it. To Green Street's credit though, they adjusted my bill accordingly.

Green Street isn't the cheapest place, but hey, if you're on an expense account . . .

McQUEENS UPSTAIRS

317 - 10 Avenue S.W. 269-4722

Sun, open 5pm for dinner; Mon-Sat, open 5:30pm for dinner; Mon-Fri, 11:30am - 2pm. Reservations recommended. Fully licensed. Non-smoking section. V, M, AE, ER, DC. Live blues & jazz Tues-Sat evenings. Dance floor. Moderate-expensive.

Cannery Row has been around a while, carving out a reasonable niche with seafood. A few years ago, they opened McQueens Upstairs at their 10th Avenue location. McQueens rates right near the top as one of Calgary's prettier restaurants. Dark mahogany walls are offset by tiny spotlights and deep-blue lamps. A skylight spills sunshine into the room during lunch and the city's glow during dinner. The place exudes a grainy elegance like something out of a Bogart movie. Black and white clad staff enhance this image with their demure helpfulness. They aren't overly speedy, but they are friendly.

McQueens has grown and matured since it first opened — the food now matches the surroundings in terms of quality. Everything on the menu is tempting, as are the daily specials. They're crossing culinary lines to bring new light to fresh seafood. There are escargots Pernod, prawns with a miso (Japanese paste of fermented soybeans and rice) and mustard sauce, blackened snapper, and ceviche (a Latin American recipe of shrimp and scallops marinated in lime juice). They serve a dynamite spinach salad in the evening that's dressed with warm, tender scallops poached in raspberry vinaigrette. Past specials include New Zealand orange roughy sautéed with papaya purée and smoked Winnipeg goldeye with a lemon and garlic butter. For those whose tastes run more to turf than surf, there is a handful of red meat dishes, although most of them are combined with seafood.

I decided to try one of the basics — clam chowder. A buttery Boston-style. Creamy and lots of clams, it had me dipping my crusty roll into it (discreetly of course). While I was debating whether to order a refill and another roll, my main course arrived — huge Digby scallops sautéed with cream, curry, raisins, and slivered almonds. It was prime scallop season, and these ones were done perfectly, their springy tenderness offset by the leathery raisins and crunchy almonds. The yellow curry sauce enhanced the scallops without drowning out their flavour. A few brussel sprouts and a mound of saffron rice on the side, and I was as happy as a clam.

There's a delicate request on the menu for customers to refrain from smoking pipes or cigars. This is smart because, although there is a non-smoking section, the heavy tobaccos would detract horribly from the food.

With some vintage blues in the background, a nice glass of wine, and great seafood, McQueens transports you from landlocked Calgary to the port of your choice. My only disappointment is that their long staircase leads to a parking lot instead of a dock.

STEPPS

880 - 16 Avenue S.W. (Mount Royal Village) 228-0303

Mon-Sat, 11am - to late night. Reservations preferred.
Fully licensed. Non-smoking section. V, M, AE. Lounge.
Summer outdoor dining. Moderate.

When I first heard there was a restaurant called Stepps, I thought, "Great. A Russian restaurant." Upon closer inspection, I found that it had nothing to do with the steppes of Russia and everything to do with the steps of Mount Royal Village. Located on the top floor of the shopping complex, it is accessible by elevator, escalator, or a steep set of steps off 8th Street.

The spot was formerly a crêperie that had some of the worst service and poorest food in the city. Stepps, however, bears no relation to the former place. It's efficient and friendly and serves food that's not bad.

Stepps is a sprawling space decorated in the sensitive green and pink pastels of the mid '80s. Having one of the few outdoor cafés above ground level in Calgary, dining outdoors here can be quite pleasant if you can handle the glare. It's bright and cheery, the kind of restaurant where you expect to see the cast from *LA Law* "doing" lunch.

It has a menu that fits too, a crossbreed of Californian and Continental. I don't think there is really a label for it. Eclectic, I guess. The fare is quite recognizable — fillet of sole, spinach salad, escargots — but things are done just a little differently. The sole is poached in champagne, the escargots are prepared with blue cheese, the spinach salad is dressed with oysters. The lunch menu predominantly offers salads like papaya with shrimp or greens with chicken and cashews and sandwiches like Ruebens with a peppercorn sauce or chicken with a Mexican mole sauce, each for well under $10. The bulk of Stepps' business is created by the lunch and shopping crowds, but it's open for dinner too. Dinner moves a bit upscale with beef in blueberry pepper sauce or veal with wild mushrooms. But prices are still okay, the most expensive entrée being $14.95.

I started my lunch with two thick slices of smoked salmon mousse — a touch dry, but with a nice smoked salmon taste and lots of crusty baguette. My partner's daily soup of puréed potatoes and leeks was full of flavour and thick enough to hold up a spoon, yet not artificially thickened.

Our main-course sandwiches were quite acceptable. The Bookmaker was a high-tone steak sandwich of good quality. The hot turkey on baguette was quite tasty — warm smoked turkey was covered in a creamy sage sauce. For me, the sauce went well with the poultry, but it may be too much for some. And it was nice to see decent-sized pieces of watermelon and cantaloupe as garnishes. (All sandwiches come with a choice of Caesar salad or french fries.)

I have to mention what for me is the most unusual aspect of Stepps: The tables are covered in padded vinyl. This is great for leaning elbows or pounding fists, but nothing slides on them, be it cutlery, plates, or glasses full of water. So if you're a glass slider like me, be careful. Or more importantly, if you're *with* a glass slider like me, watch out.

DELIS, DINERS & BISTROS

BLACKFOOT TRUCK STOP

1840 - 9 Avenue S.E. 265-5964

Sun-Sat, 24 hours a day (closed Christmas Day).
Reservations accepted. Beer & wine. Non-smoking section.
V, M, PetroCanada card. Take-out. Cheap.

If you're looking for the smokiest place in Calgary to eat, the Blackfoot Truck Stop is probably your cup of tea (or tray of ashes). It doesn't matter that they have a non-smoking section, this place seems to attract a clientele that can overpower any bylaw or air-conditioner. It's so smoker-oriented that when things are slow, they just shut down the non-smoking section.

That's too bad because the air quality gets in the way of what is really a pretty fair diner. Long considered the classic in Calgary, the Blackfoot is renowned for its six-inch tall flapper pie. No matter that five of these inches are meringue, it's still good. All the food here is basic — hot meat sandwiches, cold sandwiches to-go, a selection of your favourite canned soups, breakfast all day. The Blackfoot serves the best side bacon in town. Their pancakes, though a little gooey, will carry you miles down the road. The hot turkey sandwich is bland, but certainly the equal of any my mother ever made.

Service is fast, but sometimes uneven. On one occasion our waitress smiled a lot, but arbitrarily deleted the roll from my dinner special. Maybe it was because the group of guys in the Fruehauf hats were giving her a hard time. (Chauvinism lives, perhaps preserved in smoke, at the Blackfoot.)

They still have those anatomically correct portraits of eighteen-wheelers — little holes have been cut which allow lights to shine through where they would on the real things. The perfect decoration for a diner shrine like this.

BUZZARDS CAFÉ

140 - 10 Avenue S.W. 264-6959

Mon-Sat, 11:30am - 10pm. Reservations recommended for dinner. Fully licensed. Non-smoking section. V, M, AE, DC. Pub. Summer outdoor dining. Cheap-moderate.

Buzzards Café has gained a well-earned reputation as one of Western Canada's best watering holes. It started out as a small eatery and wine bar. But although they still offer one of the better wine lists in Calgary, beer has definitely taken over.

The adjoining Bottlescrew Bill's Old English Pub serves 130 kinds of beer at any given time. Like the Chimay Grande Reserve made by Trappist monks in Belgium. Or their own Buzzard Breath Ale brewed exclusively for them by Big Rock in Calgary (but now exported to thristy Americans). With dart boards, cozy corners, and non-stop sports television, the pub is a civilized place to quaff an ale.

The food at Buzzards has improved significantly over the years. The lunchtime menu, like the menu in the pub, is an attractive collection of burgers, bunwiches, salads, and stir-fries — a light to moderately heavy version of good pub food. By the time this book is out, Buzzards will have converted to a prawn house in the evenings. There will be garlic prawns, Sambuca prawns, prawns in tomato sauce with feta cheese, honey prawns, and bacon-wrapped prawns. Other beef and chicken dishes will be available, but the old bird will definitely have a crustacean look.

Buzzards recently had a facelift with new carpet and new oak dividers that give it a cozier feel. They also have one of the best patios going. Facing west and south and nicely sheltered, I've sat out there during a February chinook and been quite comfy. Although it has a view of the railroad tracks and busy 1st Street, the trees and general ambience make it a pleasant place.

Irrepressible owner and wine writer Stuart Allan is always on the bandwagon of the latest food and drink trend, bringing his customers the best for the best price. Buzzards is the kind of place where you can be a regular. It's the closest place to *Cheers* that we have in Calgary.

EARL'S TIN PALACE

2401 - 4 Street S.W. 228-4141

Sun, 10:30am - midnight; Mon-Wed, 11am - 1am;
Thurs-Sat, 11am - 2am. Reservations not accepted. Fully
licensed. Non-smoking section. V, M, AE. Lounge.
Summer outdoor dining. Sunday à la carte brunch.
Cheap-moderate.

I'm fascinated by formula restaurants. The ones with themes and branch offices and corporate structures that rival IBM. One such place is Earl's, a chain that has managed to attract a huge market share with its attitude, ambience, and willingness to change with the times. Ever since my first chips and gravy in the all-night orange and purple Fuller's of yester-year, I knew these people had a real niche.

Earl's has come a long way from the fluorescent Fuller's decor and the days of stuffed birds and umbrellas. During the Olympics, Earl moved into a whole new plane with his Tin Palace. This place is right out of West Edmonton Mall. It's a huge square building with tons of glass and sandstone arches imported from Mexico. And there's a stunning fountain outside (that's great — we don't have nearly enough fountains in this town). It's a bold location for Earl's. This is not the typical, high traffic street with furniture warehouses and polyester chain restaurants. This is 4th Street, where they go up against the Rose and Entre Nous and St. Tropez. For once, you have to look at Earl's seriously.

Once you're through the heavy glass doors with clumsy wrought-iron handles, the interior of the Tin Palace is no less impressive than the exterior. It's one huge room with a high ceiling, dark plaster walls, and three areas — smoking, non-smoking, and La Bar. It's so big and busy that customers are tempted to just stand in the foyer wondering what to do. The vaguely generic decor — sort of a Southern U.S. or Spanish-style — engulfs patrons in a combination grand ballroom and train station atmosphere. Intimacy is lost in the incredible noise. Sounds bounce off the hard surfaces while music tries to seep through. But that same noise does provide for privacy — you can't possibly understand what anyone else is saying, sometimes including the people at your own table.

Speaking of tables, the booths are a hoot. It looks like someone forgot to measure the height of the benches. If you're tall, fine. But if not, go for a table with chairs. The booth benches are so low that you feel like a four year old without a booster seat as you look up at the table.

I've always been impressed with Earl's service. It sometimes gets a little smarmy for me, but if I turned over as many tables as those waiters do during a shift, I'd want to hold onto my tips too — this can be a very lucrative job. They may not know very much about food, but they do know how to sling it out, keep you happy, and solve problems immediately.

And then there is Earl's food. In a word, it's Big. You get a real faceful of decent fare for a reasonable price. It's fresh, quite tasty, and fairly nonchallenging with burgers, steaks, soups, and salads. It's also very '90s in its mixture of cuisines. There's tomato-basil crostini, there's fettuccine with prawns in ginger-oyster sauce, there's guacamole, and there's chicken satay with peanut sauce.

Perhaps the most stunning thing about the Tin Palace is the clientele. This is not ball jackets and golf pants. This is uptown. Heavy-duty gold bangles over Adrienne Vittadini ensembles. Double-breasted blazers with scarlet pocket poofs. Two-hundred dollar shades and $80 haircuts. Who are these people? They look like they should be hanging out in a fine French restaurant. But they're at Earl's Tin Palace. And they're having fun. And they're coming back.

I have to take my hat off to Earl. If you can't get the Mount Royalites to Macleod Trail, bring Macleod Trail to Mount Royal.

The other locations are: 10333 - Southport Road S.W. (252-9928), 3012 - 17 Avenue S.E. (273-3275), 315 - 8 Avenue S.W. (265-3275), 335 Toronto-Dominion Square (262-6577), and 1110 - 16 Avenue N.W. (289-2566).

4 ST. ROSE

2116 - 4 Street S.W. 228-5377

Sun, 10am - midnight; Mon-Thurs, 8am - midnight; Fri, 8am - 1am; Sat, 10am - 1am. Reservations not accepted. Fully licensed. Non-smoking section. V, M, AE. Lounge. Summer outdoor dining. Cheap-moderate.

Once a quiet little flower on a barren street, the Rose has blossomed and grown into a flourishing garden. It would have been good enough to just stay as that cute little renovated house. But now there is the General Store, Pasta Frenzy, and two sidewalk cafés. The amazing thing is that the quality has remained high. Like any place their size, however, they're completely capable of poor service and mediocre food from time to time, but those lineups aren't for nothing.

You can still order some of the items that opened the place — at not significantly higher prices either. Their burger remains the quintessential deli treat. They've added more *au courant* dishes like a Thai spinach salad and a Cajun chicken pizza to keep the menu timely, but the Caesar salad and the BLT are as good as ever. The quesadillas rival anything found in Mexican restaurants. I'm a fan of their tomato-basil soup, a simple preparation of fresh, natural ingredients. It goes nicely with the cream cheese and fresh basil on baguette. The carrot cake is still dense and gooey with cream cheese icing, and the turtle pie is rich with pecans, chocolate, and caramel.

The Rose is loud and crowded and a model of its kind. With all those extra seats, I'm surprised the lineups are still so long. But I guess that's the product of being good.

HUGO'S DELI CAFE

1511 - Centre B Street N.W. 276-4896

*Sun-Wed, 8:30am - 10pm; Thurs-Sat, 8:30am - 11:30pm.
Reservations recommended for lunch. Beer & wine. Non-
smoking section. V, M. Take-out. Summer outdoor dining.
Cheap-moderate.*

I don't typically look behind the parking lot of the North Centre Inn
(formerly the Beacon) for good restaurants. In fact it's not advisable to
look back there for much of anything. But if you do, you'll find a great
new restaurant called Hugo's. Formerly dubbed Hugo Boss, they've
shortened the name because of confusion with the Italian designer of the
same moniker. It's run by a fellow named Hugo who frequenters of The
Little Place in Kensington may remember as the originator of that eatery.

Hugo's calls itself a deli café, a nouvelle term for diner, and the menu
spans the globe. Big breakfasts — the bacon and egg type — pizzas,
pastas, and stir-fries take you around the world.

We started with some spring rolls, seven tubes of ground meats and
vegetables for a reasonable $3.75. They were less greasy than many, very
light, and served with both a sweet-and-sour sauce and a Vietnamese fish
sauce. I, of course, followed the rolls with the tried and true deli-diner
test, the clubhouse sandwich. Excellent ingredients: real chicken, crisp
bacon, Black Forest ham, actual cheddar, sprouts, tomato, and mayo all
crammed between thick slices of multi-grain bread. A blue-ribbon
sandwich served with very fine fries and a crunchy dill pickle. My wife's
bacon and tomato sandwich was a perfect contrast of crisp bacon and
cool tomato. Instead of fries, she tried a mixed salad with a lovely house
dressing — a simple, creamy, lemony concoction.

Not only were we surprised at the quality of the food, but at the
quantity as well. It practically fell off our plates. And the prices were
great too. The clubhouse was only $5.25, the bacon and tomato $4.50. If
you want to spend big bucks, you'll have to go for the steak and shrimp
combo, the only dish to break the $10 mark (it's $10.95). Most things are
$4 to $7. Amazing for the quality.

At these prices, you might expect scuzzy surroundings. Not so. Hugo's
is in an old building that has been crisply renovated and designed. It's
pretty and clean and air-conditioned. There's a room each for smokers
and non-smokers, and there's a nice patio. You might also expect surly
service. Again, not so. Very pleasant staff. When I commented on the
quality of the dill pickle, our waitress brought us some extra ones at no
charge. Now that's customer service.

There's nothing I can say against Hugo's. They have a great attitude to
go along with top-notch food, first-rate service, and free parking. What
more could I ask for?

HUSKY HOUSE

2525 - 32 Avenue N.E. 291-1616

Sun-Sat, 24 hours a day. Reservations not accepted. Beer
& wine. Non-smoking table. V, M, Husky card. Cheap.

Ball caps, pearl-snap buttons, "I rode the Sky Tram" sweatshirts, and weary eyes. Signs advertising fresh homestyle banana-cream pie and cinnamon buns. Place-mat maps of Canada measuring the mileage between Husky service stations. Coffee cups labeled with double H's. Menus offering the Trucker's Breakfast, the Rancher's Breakfast, and the steak sandwich special with mashed potatoes.

Welcome to the Husky House. They never close. Heck, they hardly even slow down. People don't go to the HH unless they're hungry, so the chow has to come fast.

A waitress named Betty arrives at my table with a pot of coffee and a mile-wide smile. What can she get me? Those pies look real good. But soup would fill the hole left from bumping along Highway 9. And a hamburger.

Outside, the parking lot is full of eighteen-wheelers, RV's, and license plates from far away. A burly traveler squeezes into his bug-splattered Chevy Sprint with a bag of goodies for the road. Revitalized by his BLT, chocolate cream pie, and barrel of coffee, the road looks long but easier now.

"Here's your soup, honey. Careful. It's hot." Betty's back. A bowl of beef vegetable soup steams away, full of floating alphabits and Christie's cracker crumbs.

The fellow in the Flames t-shirt lights up a Player's. Looks like it's been a long haul. The guy with the tattoos dangles a baby booty in front of his little one's face, smiling as the baby tries to grab it. The chick in the corner rants into the phone while twisting her mega-blond perm. A group with rodeo buckles and fresh bruises slides tenderly into their booth.

"Here's your hot hamburger san, hon." It's Betty again.

Crinkle-cut frozen fries and the daily vegetable of frozen peas, corn, and carrots flank the two burgers piled with mushrooms and dripping with gravy. Maybe I should've gone for the mashed. Oh well. This isn't so much food as it is fuel.

"More coffee? A piece of pie?" More smiles from Betty in her crisp blue and white uniform. All right. That third cup smooths out the last of the road wrinkles.

"How was it today sir? Not too many people write while they eat." Betty delivers the bill. It's $7.98, and I'm full. Betty gets a $3 tip. A pack of Juicy Fruit at the counter, and I'm on the road again. I wonder how far it is to the next Husky House?

JOEY'S ONLY

9250 - Macleod Trail S. (Macleod Mall) 252-7060

*Sun, 4pm - 8pm; Mon-Sat, 11am - 10pm. Reservations
not accepted. Beer & wine. Totally non-smoking on Tues,
Thurs & Sun. V, M. Take-out. Moderate.*

The original Joey's Only was, and still is, at 1411 - 17 Avenue S.W. It's
a weathered storefront with a huge deep-fryer, a long counter, and a
couple of rows of tables. There's not much decoration, and the
entertainment consists of watching the cooks flambé fish or burn
themselves on the fryer. Funny thing is, Joey doesn't own this place
anymore. He sold it off a couple of years ago to open other Joey's.

But the new ones have a similar character and attitude, albeit in more
polished settings. They have the sparse and hardy good looks of coastal
fish 'n' chip shops, with prices to match. Although costs go up and down
with the market, there's no better quality for your dollar in local seafood.

After Joey left 17th Avenue, he set up his deep-fryers in Macleod Mall.
Then, with the opening of the Northwest leg of the LRT, he popped up
on Crowchild Trail. That became so popular that just before we went to
print, he put in another place on 14th Street N.W. and bought the old
Cosmopolitan on 4th Street, dreaming of yet more Joey's. So, including a
second Macleod Trail location for take-out, there should be five of them
around. And that's not including the original. Will this guy ever stop? Or
maybe he should reconsider the name. How about Joey's Third? Or
Joey's Twelfth?

But I hope he never quits. His concept is sound — fresh fish, simply
prepared in casual, family-style, professionally friendly joints. The fish is
good whether it's poached or charbroiled or blackened or lightly battered
and deep-fried along with chips. Shrimp are crisply hot in a Cajun pan-
fry or cool in lemon butter. Go yuppie with orange roughy (originally
known as slime head according to Joey) or traditional with trout. The
french fries taste great. There are no unnecessary vegetables. And
everything slides down better with a glass of draught beer.

So whether you're into raw oysters or smoked Alaska Black cod, you
might want to drop into Joey's. And if you can't find one near you, wait a
few minutes. At his rate, there should be one along any time now.

The other locations are: 7521 - Macleod Trail S. (252-8557), 2120 -
Crowchild Trail N.W. (284-4968), 4404 - 14 Street N.W., and 2312 - 4
Street S.W. At press time, the last two locations had yet to get phone
numbers.

JUMP-START CAFÉ

155 - Glendeer Circle S.E. (Calgary Auto Centre)
259-2526 & 252-2046 (Fax)

Mon-Fri, 8am - 8pm; Sat, 8am - 4pm. Reservations accepted. Fully licensed. Non-smoking section. V, M, AE, DC. Take-out. Summer outdoor dining. Cheap-moderate.

Buying a car or getting it fixed are two anxiety-ridden experiences. Somewhere along the line you're usually offered a cup of coffee that tastes as though it was drained from a radiator. And you usually drink it since most showrooms or garages aren't surrounded by great restaurants.

But the Calgary Auto Centre is different. Aside from being a place to tune up the Beamer, it contains one of the best cafés in town, the Jump-Start. It's run by the same people who own The Roasterie, that teensy spot on 10th Street N.W. that's always packed. But the Jump-Start has more room. In fact unlike The Roasterie, there's enough space to move about easily and to create a reasonable non-smoking section.

Using Roasterie-roasted coffee, the Jump-Start pours a decent cup of java or bag of beans. But they don't stop there. They offer breakfast until 11 a.m., plus a full menu of appetizers, sandwiches, soups, salads, and more substantial entrées. And the food is good.

This in the only place in Calgary where you can dive into a good diner breakfast and drink a smooth cup of coffee at the same time. The sausages or bacon with eggs, hash browns, and toast is everything I want it to be — fresh, hot, well prepared. What else can I say? You want your eggs easy-over? That's how you get 'em. You want your bacon crisp? That's how it comes. And the hash browns. Well, they are simply the best in Calgary.

I was so impressed with the Jump-Start's breakfast that I went back for dinner several times and was equally impressed. Great daily soups — a spicy jalapeno and cheese, a thick tomatoey minestrone. Huge sandwiches piled with quality cold cuts or rolled into pitas. Big salads doused in tarragon vinaigrette or sherry mayonnaise. Entrées like chicken poached in a cream and white wine sauce over rice. (Actually, this was very good, but not the best value at $7.95 for only chicken and rice and no vegetables or salad.) All the sandwiches and burgers run the $4.95 to $6.95 range and come with a choice of fries, soup, or a very decent and very large garden salad.

The desserts are darn good too. Nanaimo bars, carrot cake, peanut butter cookies. Just the sort of things to make the price of a new brake job go down easier. (Everything looks better with a coffee and sugar glow.)

I have to compliment the staff too. They're nice people who know they're serving good food, but don't get carried away about it. One fellow even advised us as to which baked goods were fresh and which were stale. We bought some fresh goodies to-go, and he threw in a few stale Nanaimo bars for free (which were surprisingly good anyway).

With its high southern windows and outdoor patio, the Jump-Start Café is bright and cheery. The red and grey decor is largely high-tech functional, but innovative art exhibitions let you look at something. And to while away your time waiting for the dreaded estimate, there's a pile of newspapers and magazines at the back.

So next time you're kicking tires at the Calgary Auto Centre, drop by the Jump-Start. Or if you work in the area, consider getting on their fax roster. They'll fax their daily menu to your office where you can choose your meal and then fax or phone it in.

KENSINGTON'S DELICAFÉ

1414 - Kensington Road N.W. 283-0771

Sun-Sat, 10am - midnight. Reservations accepted for large groups. Fully licensed. Non-smoking section. V, M, AE. Summer outdoor dining. Sat & Sun à la carte brunch. Live music Wed-Sat evenings. Cheap-moderate.

The gentrification of the area around Kensington Road and 10th Street N.W. has not only changed the look of the buildings, it has changed the look of the inhabitants as well. No longer the home of low-rent seekers, it's given way to a more well-heeled crowd. But the last remnants of the crunchy granola crowd, mixed in with the heavy-duty hikers, can be found frequently in Kensington's Delicafé. This place is a hybrid of the '60s coffee-houses with its close, almost claustrophobic feel endemic to existential discussions over cups of steaming java. It has wood walls and heavy wood tables and a corner for live performances. There's an eclectic collection of paintings and posters on the walls with more of a tendency towards art than polemics. It's long hair gone grey, radicals grown thoughtful, flowered dresses that are fading, and Jim Morrison lives. It's warm and alive and very mature.

It's also a commercially viable restaurant that doesn't rely totally on its bean sprout atmosphere to survive. The Delicafé has something for everyone, all good and well-prepared. There are salads, soups, sandwiches, and a variety of dishes, from hummus to fettuccine to ribs. Perhaps its best known item is the Deliburger, an offering that I rated the best of its kind in Calgary a few years back. It's still right up there in 1990, freshly made with six ounces of meat and your own selection of toppings — and always a piece of Trident gum. Served with a big side of fries, it's remained consistently good over the years.

Delicafé desserts have gained a place in infamy around the waists of many a Hillhurst native — one of the prices you pay for living within walking distance. Their popular cheesecake is kept company by carrot cake, chocolate Amaretto cobbler, and a hot carrot pudding. And the coffee is plentiful.

Kensington's Delicafé is an eatery of the '90s. The portions are large, there's no cheaping out, the service is casual and congenial, and the kitchen efficient. It's a friendly stop-in on Kensington Road, one that should see in the next century.

LION'S DEN

234 - 17 Avenue S.E. 265-8482

Sun-Sat, 8am - 11pm. Reservations accepted except hockey & concert evenings. Beer, wine & liqueurs. No non-smoking section. V, M, AE. Take-out. Cheap.

The Lion's Den is one of those places you drive by all the time and never really notice. It's right across from the Stampede Grounds on 17th Avenue S.E., and it attracts great crowds whenever there's a game or major event at the grounds. It doesn't make any pretensions to gourmet food or international decor. It's a fluorescent diner with velvet paintings and a killer clubhouse. There are booths, plus one of the few legitimate lunch counters left — the kind with red vinyl swivel stools bolted to the floor and stainless steel napkin dispensers and vinegar bottles dotted along the arborite. It's not one of those nouveau lunch counters. It's right out of the '50s with diner plates and glasses and industrial-strength cutlery. The Lion's Den is as homey as my rumpus room and just about as homely. The painting of Pancho Villa would look great over my wet bar.

You can look through the rectangular delivery window in the back and see the boss, Lidia Festa (better known as Mamma), cooking up a storm. Two big soup pots sit out front where manager/waiter/son Enrico keeps the utensils. I tried Lidia's onion soup one day. It wasn't one of those fancy varieties that took a week and a half to make and was priced accordingly. This was a solid soup, packed with onions, and priced at $1.50. After Enrico scooped it out of the pot, he covered it in a double layer of homemade croutons and a pile of parmesan. It didn't have any of those horrible, gooey strings of mozzarella.

I also ordered one of the higher priced items, the "chicken roar." Pieces of chicken and veal in a cream and white wine sauce had been poured into and over a puff pastry shell. It was very creamy with a nice light taste. Not a landmark of cuisine, but for $6, who can argue? Especially with a huge side of golden french fries. These fries were big, freshly cut chunks of deep-fried potatoes that I'd rate among the best in the city.

The clubhouse sandwich is arguably among the best too. Thick slices of freshly roasted turkey, crisp bacon, big slices of tomato, crunchy lettuce, mayonnaise, three pieces of toasted whole-grain bread. So simple, yet often done so badly elsewhere.

It's obvious that the Festas care. They're not trying to expand anyone's culinary horizons, but they won't serve you anything that they themselves wouldn't eat. Whether Lidia is making lasagna or schnitzel or an egg salad sandwich, they're serving good, fresh food at cheap prices. And along the way, there's a little entertainment. Enrico is an endless source of really bad jokes — between laughs, you can watch his favourite programs on a TV that is strategically placed by the soup pots.

So I like the Lion's Den — velvet paintings, fluorescent lights, and all. I like the fact that they're open every day from 8 a.m. until 11 p.m., and I'm amazed that Lidia is in the kitchen for that entire time. That kind of dedication is incredible.

Dinner for two will be between $10 and $20. It's not the fanciest place in town, but it's one of the most honest.

PHIL'S

2312 - 16 Avenue N.W. (Motel Village) 284-9696

June-mid Sept: Sun-Sat, 6am - 11pm. Mid Sept-May: Sun-Sat, 6am - 9pm. Phone for reservations. Beer & wine. Non-smoking section. V, M, AE. Cheap.

Cars whiz by on 16th Avenue heading to Banff. Across the parking lot a ten-year-old boy bounces on the motel bed while his father takes a short walk for ice. Saturday ski-morning pancakes. Late night caffeine. Trans-Canada weariness washed away with an open Denver and a bowl of soup. This is Phil's. It used to be Phil's Pancake House. Now it's just plain Phil's, as in Phil's Industries of Canada Ltd., with ten locations across Alberta serving breakfast all day long.

I would think Phil's chicken burgers, his fish and chips, his liver and onions, and his BLT or grilled cheese are all good. But I don't know because I've never gotten past the pancakes, no matter what time I've been there. Whether buttermilk, buckwheat, potato, or what have you, they're always hot and just the right consistency to smother in whipped butter and maple syrup. So-o-o good. Pancakes need eggs, and Phil's serves them up any way you like. Even as a Benedict with hash browns. But they're best over-easy with the pancakes.

Phil's is a basic kind of place with a basic kind of menu for people who don't want surprises. They want a table now, their food in a minute, and their coffee cup full always. And that's what Phil's does best. The decor hasn't changed in a while and probably won't in this millennium. There are the same vinyl booths, the same comforting green and brown interior, the same cafeteria dishes, and the same smiling staff. And that's okay, as long as the food stays the same. We need places like Phil's for Saturday morning ski trips and days on the road that are too long.

There are three other Calgary locations: 907 - Glenmore Trail S.W. (252-6061), 3210 - 17 Avenue S.E. (272-1007), and 1520 - 14 Street S.W. (244-1850).

PIAZZA STEAK HOUSE

1637 - 37 Street S.W. 246-4664

Sun, noon - 11pm; Mon-Thurs, 11am - 1am; Fri & Sat, 11am - 2am. Reservations accepted. Fully licensed. Non-smoking section. V, M, AE. Lounge. Take-out. Summer outdoor dining. Cheap-moderate.

There's a guy at work who, every six months or so, quizzes me on where to take his wife for a special occasion. I rummage around in my brain, ask him a few probing questions, and come up with some terribly brilliant ideas. A few days later I ask him where he went, and he tells me that, after much discussion with his wife, they went to the Piazza Steak House. I finally figured if I couldn't get him to take my suggestions, the least I could do was try his Piazza. I did, and I liked it.

I love a nice honest meal — big Greek salads packed with feta cheese and onions and olives, huge burgers oozing with cheese, ribs so thick and sticky that you can't stand to watch the guy at the next table suck on them. Piazza doesn't do anything fancy. They just do it well. From the pizzas that are served on funny stainless steel, pedestalled trays (I guess so you can load more food underneath) to the salads so huge that they fall off the plates, everything comes out fresh and tasty.

Piazza is one of your great neighborhood eatery stories. A little family place that started in 1972 by making pizzas and grilling steaks, they've added a lounge, renovated the dining room, put in a sunroom and a deck, and now it's huge. The main dining room, filled with booths and tables, has an overstuffed rumpus room look and an amazing collection of popsicle stick sculptures. It's busy and bustling and packed with energy, especially when there's a Flames game on the TV in the corner. The staff moves constantly, setting and resetting tables, hustling out pizzas and heaping plates of food. But the warm, friendly atmosphere is still there. Our waitress was a darling lady who could be your aunt. I felt guilty not finishing my salad — I thought she'd tell my mother. And when our first two wine choices were unavailable, she brought us a bottle of retsina because she thought we'd like it.

We tried their souvlaki (after all, they're a Greek family), which came on a mammoth platter. Two skewers of marinated and broiled pork on a king-sized bed of rice were served with a bowl of tangy tzatziki sauce and a side of excellent Greek salad. For $9.75, just a heck of a meal. My only problem was that I couldn't eat anything else. My partner pigged out on the bacon burger, a classic, old-fashioned "Big Burger." Six ounces of good beef was stuffed into a kaiser and piled with tomatoes, onions, lettuce, lots of cheddar, and thick slices of back bacon. If the side of fries doesn't grab you, they'll exchange it for yogurt and fruit.

There are oodles of other dishes, from calamari to barbecued chicken, manicotti to sirloin steaks. And don't forget the garlic toast and fried mushrooms for big appetites.

What else can I say? I don't think Piazza would be my first choice for a special occasion or a quiet tête-à-tête, but for a big feed and a hockey game, it's right up there.

THE SOUP KITCHEN

738 - 17 Avenue S.W. 228-3667

Mon-Sat, 10am - 8pm. Reservations not accepted. Unlicensed. Totally non-smoking. No credit cards. Takeout. Summer outdoor dining. Cheap.

I remember when 17th Avenue was a place that parents forbade their children to tread. Fifteen to twenty years ago it was pretty much a collection of worn out old houses with lots of loud music and long hair. But it changed, thanks partly to the pioneering efforts of places like the Prairie Dog Inn, Bagels & Buns, and The Soup Kitchen. Although these places appealed to the loud music, long hair crowd, they also drew in a lot of people who saw the potential of the area. And look at it now. All trendy and neat. And amazingly, the Prairie Dog Inn (now called Buon Giorno), Bagels & Buns, and The Soup Kitchen are still around. The Soup Kitchen is still the most '60s-looking of the three with its roughhewn wood and devotion to vegetarianism. And it still packs in the faithful every day. The hair is a little shorter and thinner, and there are more BMW's than VW vans, but the clientele continues to dive into the low fat, low salt, no meat cuisine.

It's set up cafeteria-style. Regular dishes and daily specials are outlined on overhead boards, and you line up to place your order. A coffee pot steams away on one side, a bubble of mineral water burbles on the other.

True to its name, The Soup Kitchen offers three or four daily soups, all vegetable-based. I tried a spicy black bean chowder, thick with carrots, cauliflower, turnip, and black beans. Served in a large ceramic bowl with the daily bread creation, it's a meal in itself. The bread that day was an unusual roll of soy flour, rice flour, and blue cornmeal — very dense, a little bland, but okay when smeared with butter. I also tried a hot sandwich of tomato, mushroom, and cheddar cheese on a large slab of unsalted whole-grain bread. Served with a side salad of organically grown vegetables in a tahini dressing, I felt real wholesome by the end of my meal.

The Soup Kitchen's food does taste good. It's a change for a meat eater like me, but it's expertly prepared by the former chef of Menta, the former oddball eatery on 11th Avenue. Never the most popular restaurant in town, Menta did generate an avid following with its unique cuisine. Now, within the confines of The Soup Kitchen's philosophy, this same creativity comes through.

The place is not at all formal. The staff don't care if the bread is cut a little crooked, as long as it's fresh and healthy. And the customers don't mind standing in line with their red trays and then squashing behind wobbly arborite tables to sit in church pews. It's a calm place with comforting food, very much the product of a different time.

There's not a lot more to say about The Soup Kitchen. It's a restaurant that is very assured of itself because it's been around so long and because no one has been able to replicate it. It's a simple, straightforward bit of '60s consciousness that only a few years ago appeared dated, but now seems to fit into the greening '90s.

SPARKY'S DINER

1006 - 11 Avenue S.W. 244-4888

Tues-Sun, 6pm - 2am; Mon-Fri, 11:30am - 2pm. Reservations recommended. Fully licensed. No non-smoking section. V, M, AE. Lounge. Live music nightly. Moderate.

There are lots of places in old warehouses that have renovated so much that they no longer look anything like a warehouse. Sparky's, however, looks a lot like a warehouse. It's not that there are large crates laying around. It's just that it is one large room with a bar at one end and a bandstand at the other. With its brick walls and loosely strewn tables and chairs that look like they've been plucked from some central Alberta tavern, there's a beer commercial sort of ambience. But with its high ceilings, octagonal concrete pillars, and Ansel Adams photographs, it also has that airy, artsy, Leonard Cohen look. Sparky's has become known as a great place for late evening music, ranging from R & B to Celtic to Tex-Mex Cajun genres. It's almost an "older" alternative to Electric Avenue, located (perhaps symbolically) a few blocks farther west along 11th Avenue.

Near the back is a fairly large open kitchen. The fare is pretty much what you'd expect — chicken wings, nachos, burgers, and spinach salads. But as things emerge from the kitchen, you get the idea that there is more happening back there than a deep-fryer. A closer look at the menu shows lamb chops in mustard sauce, pepper steak, pesto salad, and brie on baguette. What's going on here?

Simple. An amazingly talented chef, Patrice Durandeau, is at the helm. He's the chef that originally put Entre Nous on Calgary's culinary map. There are few better sauciers in town. His pepper steak is legend. His mustard sauce with lamb is rich, smooth, and thick with onions. His simple white wine, onion, and parsley sauce with steamed mussels entices me to mop up the last drops with his dense, lightly leavened bread. (And this is a place where you *can* mop your plate.) His green peppercorn pâté is a plate-filling slab with a side of pickled gherkins. This is real French-bistro food. And it's priced so well. The triple lamb chop dish with fettuccine is about ten bucks. A blue plate special of jambalaya laden with mussels, Italian sausage, shrimp, and chicken breast was $6.95.

Sparky's may be the best kept food secret in town. But don't expect to drop by for a quiet dinner at nine in the evening. Shortly after this, the music starts (with a cover charge in effect), and you might feel silly dining among all the partiers. Besides, you may not be able to breathe from all the smoke. But for lunch or an early dinner, Sparky's is a great place to dine — as long as Chef Durandeau is in the kitchen.

EAST INDIAN

MEELEN OMAR KHAYYAM

1935 - 32 Avenue N.E. 291-3188

Sun, 11am - 9pm; Mon-Thurs, 4:30pm - 10:30pm; Fri &
Sat, 4:30pm - 11pm; Mon-Fri, 11:30am - 2pm.
Reservations recommended. Fully licensed. Non-smoking
section. V, M, AE, ER, DC. Take-out. Sun à la carte
brunch. Moderate.

You can find some pretty unpleasant all-you-can-eat buffet lunches around town. You can also find some fairly awful places to eat in the light industrial section along 32nd Avenue N.E. So the Meelen Omar Khayyam Restaurant is a double surprise. Not only is it a treasure of East Indian foods, it has one of the best lunch buffets going.

Among the printing houses and automotive shops in the area, the exterior of the Meelen is fairly non-descript. Inside I'd expect to find a soup and sandwich shop filled with workers chowing down quickly before heading back to work. Instead the door is blocked by a four-foot brass rice cooker, and the air is rich with aromas from the tandoor oven. Lunchers are grazing through a buffet of cold and hot dishes.

I anticipated a lunch of middle-of-the-road, medium-spiced East Indian food where everything tasted the same. Although the dishes were spiced in the medium range, I was impressed with the variety of tastes and the overall quality of the spread. On the cold side there were bananas marinated with lemon juice and spices, an East Indian beet salad, and a kachumber salad of cucumbers and tomatoes with coriander, green chilies, and ginger. Very clean, brisk food. The hot selections included the tandoori naan bread, another bread stuffed with ground vegetables, saffron rice, and seasoned zucchini. A dal mixture combined three kinds of beans, and there was another vegetarian mélange of seven vegetables. The meats included lamb meatballs in a reddish yogurt sauce, a dish of ground lamb and peas, and a delicious tandoori chicken that had marinated for twelve hours before cooking. Off to the side there were also little spiced rice crackers called papadums and deep-fried vegetable fritters called pakoras, made with black chick pea flour.

An excellent buffet. Every dish retained its integrity because each was presented in a small individual tray that emptied quickly, only to be instantly replaced by a new one. Occasionally the wait for naan was a little long but understandable.

In the evening, the Meelen produces more dishes and displays a greater depth of seasoning. Lunch and dinner focus on the Mogul Emperors' cuisine of northern and central India. But with three chefs from different parts of India, they can achieve an exciting diversity. On Sundays from 11 a.m. to 4 p.m., they hold a brunch of southern Indian foods. Items like the large crêpe dishes called dossa and the spiced soups known as sambhar are featured. Very unusual for Calgary.

The Meelen's menu also includes a lengthy description of Eastern herbs and their uses. It's good to know that all the garlic I've consumed is a general antidote for what ails me, that ginger root will make my liver feel better, and that lovage is a powerful laxative. The things one learns at dinner.

MOTI MAHAL

507 - 17 Avenue S.W. 228-9990

Sun-Sat, open 5:30pm for dinner; Mon-Fri, 11:30am - 1:30pm. Reservations required. Fully licensed. No non-smoking section. V, M, AE. Moderate.

A distinctly different Indian restaurant in our community is the Moti Mahal. It presents a very refined approach to northern Indian food, with its Moglai and Kashmiri specialties rich in cream and deep, yet subtle in spicing. The menu offers an extensive collection with exceptional quality. It includes eleven chicken, fifteen lamb, and six prawn dishes. There are also vegetable, lentil, and fish dishes, tandoori meats, stuffed breads, and birianis of seasoned basmati rice with your choice of meat, all explained nicely.

One specialty is panir, a mild homemade cheese cooked in almond sauce or cream and tomatoes or herbs and spices. We tried some as an appetizer, sliced into fingers and coated in a reddish yogurt batter before being deep-fried. The taste was light, piqued by a cool mint dip. The chicken samosas that followed were not at all greasy, a fate that often befalls these little pouches. They were full of chicken and vegetables and encased in a crisp coating. Excellent.

Our main courses of chicken Kashmiri and lamb vindaloo both used lean, tender meat in abundance. The chicken floated in a thick, yellow cream with apples, raisins, and mild spices. Incredibly good. On the opposite end, the lamb vindaloo (which is actually a southern dish) crinkled my brow after only two bites. Living up to its billing, it was wonderfully, almost excessively hot. The lamb and potatoes in it were singed by the rusty brown sauce. With basmati rice and hot naan bread, the only other thing I needed was a couple of cold brews.

Staff are pretty good, clarifying any unusual dishes and procedures. But the night we last visited, they wouldn't pull two tables together to accommodate a party of six.

Moti Mahal's only real drawback is that the smallness of the place doesn't provide for a non-smoking section. The space itself is subtly decorated in an East Indian style, so it's nice albeit a little smoky at times. But if I ever have the vindaloo again, I'll be able to blow some smoke right back.

TAJ MAHAL

4816 - Macleod Trail S. 243-6362

Sun, 11:30am - 2:30pm, 5pm - 9pm; Mon-Thurs, 5pm - 11pm; Fri & Sat, 5pm - midnight; Mon-Fri, 11:30am - 2pm. Reservations recommended. Fully licensed. Non-smoking section. V, M, AE, ER, DC. Dirty Duck Pub. Take-out. Sun buffet brunch. Moderate.

The Taj has stood the test of time as Calgary's longest lived East Indian eatery. It has retained its popularity by offering good quality across a broad menu. It's perhaps not the most adventurous East Indian place, but the basics are covered well.

They specialize in northern Indian cuisine, so many dishes are cooked in their tandoor oven. Things like chicken or prawns or lamb or fish. These are marinated in various Indian spices and skewered on long pokers to then lower into the oven, which is charcoal fuelled to extreme temperatures. If you're curious, they'll take you into the kitchen to show you the procedure. Some of the bread is cooked in it too. Discs of dough are flattened with the hands and then pressed against the clay wall. They bubble and bake for a minute or two and emerge crisp and steaming. Brushed with butter before serving, they're lovely.

My vegetarian friends tell me that East Indian restaurants are among their favourites — it's one cuisine that doesn't leave them out. Although some of the Taj's dishes include dairy products like cream or butter, others are totally vegetarian, and all are available in incremental levels of spicing. The khumb is a combination of fresh mushrooms cooked with onions, tomatoes, and potatoes and topped with cilantro. Ordered medium, it's pungent enough for me, just leaving a little after-tingle. And it's priced right too, at $6.95. There's a raft of other vegetarian specialties, like cauliflower with peas and potatoes or black beans cooked in cream.

I always enjoy the Taj Mahal's samosas, served with a cooling mango chutney and a spritely hot mint sauce for dipping. The veggie ones contain chunks of spiced potato, carrot, and peas all wrapped into a pastry triangle and then deep-fried. Ground beef is used in the meat samosas.

Their murgh malai is a creamy concoction of boneless chicken in a curried yogurt sauce. The flavour is good, the chicken is tender, and you can order it as hot as you'd like. (I once took a friend to the Taj who ordered his meat extra hot. Last time I saw him that cold January evening, he was sweating profusely in the parking lot.)

The Taj is usually a quiet, peaceful departure from other Macleod Trail eateries. The two basement rooms are spacious and glittering with Indian decor. Even if the staff are occasionally confused or distracted and won't serve half-orders or substitutions, the Taj Mahal is a pleasurable experience.

TANDOOR

1147 - 17 Avenue S.W. 245-5553

Tues-Sun, 5pm - 10:30pm; Mon-Fri, 11:30am - 2pm.
Reservations recommended. Fully licensed. Non-smoking
section. V, M, AE. Take-out. Summer outdoor dining.
Moderate.

I've been accused of only liking spicy food. I don't think that's true. I like practically any kind of food, with the exception of yogurt straight-up, green peppers, and Velveeta. But I do admit that occasionally I like the big blast of flavour that comes from East Indian food. There aren't more than a handful of East Indian restaurants in town, but we're fortunate because all of them are quite good. One that has been gaining a loyal following is the Tandoor Restaurant on 17th Avenue.

It has a charming decor done in ivory and rose, the legacy of a former French tenant. These colours add a richness to the room which is highlighted by Indian tapestries and memorabilia. The separation for smokers and non-smokers is excellent, with smokers channeled to the right and non-smokers to the left — never the twain shall breath each other's air.

The kitchen is tucked into the back and houses a tandoor oven — a large metal cube with a hole in the top. Inside is a cooking chamber lined with clay bricks. Charcoal burns in the bottom, holding the temperature at roughly 500°F. Many of the house specialties (like chicken marinated in yogurt, garlic, ginger, and vinegar) are placed on long skewers and cooked in the chamber along with various breads that are pressed against the wall for about two minutes. The tandoor provides an intense heat that cooks quickly without oil. Meats don't dry out since they've been marinated, and they pick up an almost smoky taste.

Aside from their tandoor specials, they offer a wide range of other dishes prepared with curries or chilies or spices or even coconut. There are chicken, lamb, beef, and fish creations, as well as a good collection of vegetarian fare.

We opted for the broadest range possible, ordering a plate of "assorted Indian snacks" to start. Our samosa, one of those dough triangles, was stuffed with a spiced mixture of potatoes, peas, and carrots. Ground beef had been squeezed around a tandoor skewer to create a Seekh kabob — good except for too much salt. A boneless piece of chicken tikka was redolent with spices like turmeric, cumin, and cinnamon. A pile of vegetable pakoras (fritters) had been battered and deep-fried. This combo appetizer is a skillful introduction to Indian food for novices.

For veterans and the downright gluttonous, there is the "Tandoori Dinner" — eleven dishes served on a huge steel platter. That's what I had. Lamb, prawns, chicken, another beef kabob. All were baked in the tandoor, yet each retained its own flavour. The prawns were quite bizarre. Marinated overnight in various spices, they were beet red throughout. They had a balanced, savoury taste, but were very strange looking. There was also rice, mixed vegetables in a light curry, a cooling chutney, a big nan, and the painfully sweet dessert, gulab jamun (these deep-fried and syrup-dipped cheese balls are just too much for my teeth). This was a big feed with tons of spices and tastes jumping around in my mouth. But in spite of ordering it at the top end of the spice scale, I didn't find it overpowering.

A few questions about the food to one of the staff elicited an invitation to the kitchen to view preparation. This is common in East Indian eateries where the cooks display great pride in their fare. And just standing in the kitchen, breathing in all the spices, is worth the visit itself.

FRENCH

ENTRE NOUS

2206 - 4 Street S.W.   228-5525

Tues-Sat, 6pm - 10:30pm; Tues-Fri, 11:30am - 2pm.
Reservations recommended. Fully licensed. No non-
smoking section. V, M, AE, ER, DC. Moderate.

Entre Nous has been around since the mid '80s, but it changed
owners in the spring of '89. About that time, a new and excellent chef
arrived. The food at Entre Nous has always been superb, but longtime
fans will now notice a change in style to a more northern, Île de France,
Normandy fashion.

The decor hasn't changed. It's a long, rectangular room with the high,
tin-tooled ceiling painted burgundy. This colour flows down the walls
and around huge mirrors that give the illusion of more space than there
really is. In keeping with a Parisian-bistro ambience, the tables are close
to each other, and depending on your mood, you'll feel comforted by the
crowd or pressed by claustrophobia. The open kitchen takes up one-
third of the room, allowing customers to see all the action and smell all
the wonderful aromas. A collection of music ranging from Piaf to Julio
mixes with the conversation to create a certain warmth. And with that
open kitchen, it's not just an emotional warmth either — I've been hot
on every visit, whether it was July or January. So don't wear wool.

The main attraction at Entre Nous is the food. The chef is very adept.
Even a pan of fried mushrooms tastes like an exotic delicacy. His smoked
duck salad with grapefruit, pink peppercorns, and endive in vinaigrette is
impressive. Almost sour to the initial taste, it's a bizarre blend of flavours
that wakes up your mouth.

And your mouth needs preparation. Dishes like leg of lamb with a
grainy Meaux mustard sauce are not to be taken lightly. Thin slices of
lamb are sculpted over sautéed eggplant into a re-creation of Mont St.
Michel, a cathedral perched on a rock off the coast of Normandy. Swirled
about the meat is a sauce flavoured deeply enough to match the lamb.

I can't resist cassoulet. I don't know why — it's just a casserole of
beans and meats, not a whole lot different than my childhood dinners of

weiners and beans. At Entre Nous, a huge pot arrives steaming with beans, duck, sausage, pork rinds, and beef salami. It's a hearty, pungent meal — easily better than all the versions but one that I've tasted in the Languedoc region of southern France, the home of cassoulet. But they could loose the salami as far as I'm concerned. It's too strong for the dish. And I prefer my cassoulet with a crusted top. There are as many cassoulet recipes as there are cooks though.

Special menus are created for events such as Bastille Day and the November release of the Beaujolais Nouveau. They tell me that Monday evenings will soon be dedicated to special menus as well.

In addition to individual dishes, lunch features daily *table d'hôte* combinations of soup or salad, a main course, and dessert for a reasonable $11. With a half-litre of wine, you can eat dinner for under $60. That's not cheap, but a lot less than you'd pay for lesser food in some other restaurants. Unless you're bilingual though, remember to take your French-English dictionary along — the menus are needlessly in French only.

LA CHAUMIÈRE

121 - 17 Avenue S.E. 228-5690

Mon-Sat, 6pm - midnight; Mon-Fri, noon - 2pm.
Reservations preferred. Fully licensed. No non-smoking
section. V, M, AE, ER. Expensive.

As we were going to press, I discovered that the menu at La Chaumière was just about to undergo some major changes, thanks to the presence of a new chef. So, I am unable to present a regular review here. I would like to offer comment, however, on what appears will be a subtle, significant divergence in form for La Chaumière.

The changes are largely in the approach to what had been a fairly standard Continental cuisine. There are now more light sauces and a greater use of herbs. Unusual combinations — pesto on tenderloin, orange roughy in a red wine sauce, butter lettuce in an orange cream dressing with pickled beets — are more common. Some of the influences are "nouvelle" — the roughy, for example. Some are more earthy — prawns sautéed with fresh basil over polenta, for instance.

The dinner menu is now about one-third new, with the remaining two-thirds consisting of a "best of" collection from the old menu — like Russian caviar, escargots topped with béarnaise, veal with blue cheese in a port sauce, and duck rolled in green peppercorns. These favourites will be as comforting to regulars as the professional service and the elegant surroundings. The new items should keep people from getting bored and may attract those who like a little challenge in their food. Old or new, La Chaumière will continue to be one of Calgary's finest fine dining rooms.

LE GOURMET

5008 - Macleod Trail S. 287-2211

Mon-Sat, open 5:30pm for dinner; Mon-Fri, 11:30am - 2pm. Reservations preferred. Fully licensed. Non-smoking section. V, M, AE, ER, DC. Moderate-expensive.

Dining has changed over the last decade or two. The market now leans towards casual, ethnic, moderately priced restaurants and away from high-tone, dressy dining rooms. But once in a while it's nice to be pampered, to escape on a culinary daydream, to really Dine. One of the best places for this is Le Gourmet.

This restaurant has managed to weather Calgary's economic storms over the last ten years when many others have floundered. And it's not because they've cut corners. Instead, they've simply adhered to an unflinching commitment to quality in both food and service. The chef wisely combines his classical recipes with some of our best Canadian ingredients. There is poached B.C. salmon, roast Alberta rack of lamb, and Atlantic lobster bisque.

Le Gourmet has parlayed an unusual location into an asset. It's a homely building squeezed against a homely stretch of Macleod Trail, similar to many eateries in France whose doors open onto busy roads. What's outside is unimportant though. The contrast as you pass through the heavy oak doors is dramatic. You enter an elegant, European-flavoured room softened by an awning along one wall. Lace-fringed lamps dangle over well-appointed tables, splashing soft light onto art-covered walls. Everything speaks of understated quality (including the washrooms — perhaps the cleanest in town.)

Full French service is the vogue here with meals presented in shining trays and scooped onto heated plates at your table. They are watchful yet not annoyingly cloying, helpful yet not insistent. It's service with slick professionalism and a smile, not at all intimidating — you needn't worry that they're snickering about your wine choice back in the kitchen.

The smoked Alberta lamb on butter lettuce that we tried was superb, although the vinaigrette seemed light on the promised mint. Topped with fresh enoki mushrooms, the salad exuded an exceptional freshness. A lobster bisque was nicely tinged with cream and brandy. The veal with wild mushrooms featured Edmonton-grown lobster mushrooms the evening we visited. Unusually red in colour and rich in flavour, these mushrooms created the perfect marriage with the mouth-melting veal in cream sauce. The pheasant breast filled with forcemeat and covered in a champagne and rosehip sauce sounded wonderful, but was unfortunately unavailable that evening. As an alternative, the chicken breast deglazed with white wine and lingonberries was as tender as the veal and sweet with fruit — a more delicate version of turkey with cranberries.

We finished our evening with a cheese plate of beautiful cambozola and stilton warmed to room temperature and a brie-based German cheesecake — a fluffy cloud of cheese was sandwiched between layers of chocolate cake and served with a transparent raspberry sauce and tons of fresh raspberries. The perfect ending. And with a bill of $73 ($47 without our wine), it was excellent value for the money.

We felt refreshed and replenished after our three hour daydream, ready to slip back onto Macleod Trail with the rest of the traffic.

YERVAND'S

1137 - 17 Avenue S.W. 245-4136

Tues-Sat, open 6pm for dinner; Tues Fri, 11:30am - 2pm. Closed in August. Reservations preferred. Fully licensed. Non-smoking section. V, M, AE, ER, DC. Moderate-expensive.

Seventeenth Avenue S.W. is populated with lots of places to eat. It's an amazingly diverse area where some spots become outrageously popular while others languish in relative obscurity. One of the finest and most unknown is Yervand's, run by a gentleman of that name at the corner of 11th Street and 17th Avenue. It's a classical Continental restaurant with strong French and Swiss overtones. Yervand's specializes in service and sauces and succeeds marvelously at both.

From the outside, Yervand's doesn't look exceptional, with only a dark awning marking its spot. Inside, it's understated in its natural oak and forest-green decor, installed by Yervand himself. He has constructed a beautiful and functional telephone booth in one corner and distributed about fifteen tables throughout the rest of the room. It's a relatively tight room, but oak planters help divide and space it. Backed by Julio dripping from the stereo, Yervand's is classy without stuffiness or pretentions.

We shared a pâté of veal, pork, and goose liver. Spiked with spices, port, and Armagnac, it was piqued by the sweet onion preserve that accompanied it. We followed the pâté with appetizers of ravioli and cauliflower. The ravioli, stuffed with spinach and ricotta, was doused in a light cheese sauce. It doesn't sound like much more than Kraft Dinner, but the blending of flavours was superb. Yervand's real expertise with sauces, however, was evidenced by the cauliflower appetizer. Cauliflower is not one of my forty or fifty favourite vegetables, but sitting on strips of puff pastry and served in this creamy herb sauce, I could eat it every day.

Even after such great appetizers, our main courses were no disappointment. Pork tenderloin and apple wedges had been sautéed and then glazed with Calvados, creating a light, fruity meal. And two huge pieces of veal smothered in a mushroom-port sauce were tender enough to cut with a fork — its only problem was a sauce so rich and thick with mushrooms that it was difficult to finish. Not impossible, just difficult. Both meals came with an abundant supply of roasted potatoes and carrots.

Once we caught our collective breath, we sampled a couple of desserts created by Yervand's wife, Rima. Both the chocolate rum cake and the Napoleon (a layered concoction of strawberry jam, cream, and puff pastry) were terrific.

After all that, and a decent bottle of Cote du Rhone, you might think that we were wheeled out on trolleys. But the staff paced the whole evening so that we felt completely comfortable. Also adding to our comfort was the price-tag — $87, including the wine. Now that buys a lot of Big Macs, but this was much better.

GREEK

DEMETRIS SOUVLAKI

1241 - Kensington Road N.W. 283-0387

Sun, 4pm - 11pm; Mon-Sat, 4pm - midnight; Mon-Fri, 11am - 2:30pm. Reservations recommended. Fully licensed. No non-smoking section. V, M, AE. Take-out. Moderate.

No one has brought a Greek open kitchen to Calgary, one where patrons are invited in for a look at what's cooking. Most Greek places here do the expected dine-and-watch-the-belly-dancer routine. Somewhere on this Greek restaurant spectrum lies the simple souvlaki house concept — a diner with big plates of good food. This is what Demetris is.

It's a clean, quiet looking eatery done in the requisite blue and white. Checkered tablecloths with real flowers and plants contradict the sparse, linoleum-floored room. It's the kind of place that I look at and hope most of the effort is going into the food. And that is exactly what's going on here. If you can overlook the lackadaisical, impersonal service, you will find first-rate Greek fare.

We started with a plate of hummus, an unusually course grind of chick peas, garlic, tahini, and lemon juice. Served with hot pita bread made on the premises, it was excellent. The bread itself was a highlight — tender and chewy, not tough and leathery like we often see elsewhere. But eat it while it's warm. It goes rock hard when it cools off, suitable only for spading the garden.

Our meals of lamb souvlaki and kotopoulo lemonato (roasted lemon chicken) were just terrific. Two skewers of lamb had been marinated and drenched with herbs before grilling over an open flame, giving them a nice charbroiled flavour. They came with a small bowl of tzatziki, that tangy yogurt and cucumber dip. The chicken was so moist that it practically fell off its bones, and the skin was delicately crisp with a fresh lemon tang. Our plates were loaded down with other things too. There were piles of rice with carrots, wonderful roasted potatoes, and small herbed Greek salads. Our table reeked of Greek scents. The lamb was a reasonable $9.25 and the chicken, an incredible $6.95.

The bill of fare is typical of Greek menus around — saganaki, spanakopita, moussaka, baklava — but the preparation is carried out with such integrity. Even the pizza delivered to the table next to ours looked good.

PEGASUS

1101 - 14 Street S.W. 229-1231

Sun-Thurs, 5pm - 10:30pm; Fri & Sat, 5pm - 11:30pm; Mon-Fri, 11:30am - 2pm. Reservations recommended. Fully licensed. Non-smoking section. V, M, AE, ER. Take-out. Belly dancer Thurs-Sun evenings. Moderate.

Whenever I pass the 14th Street and 11th Avenue location of the Pegasus, I remember the fun evenings I spent there when it was the Acropol. The red and brown decor of those days gave way in the mid '80s to the full blue and white, tile and plant Greek package of the Pegasus. It's been bubbling away ever since with retsina and belly dancers.

Pegasus is more a place to have a good time than a great meal. It's busy, it's raucous, and it's fun — if you're in the right mood. If you're not, you might notice how cramped it is. And you might notice that the food is just adequate.

The house salad of cold boiled vegetables in an herbed vinaigrette is okay, but unbalanced with too much oil. The avgolemono soup is a mild bowl of chicken, lemon, and rice that I wish had more zip. The lamb fricassee with endive in lemon sauce is just as flat. But the lamb giouvetse is in a rich pot of orzo pasta and red wine sauce spiced with cloves and cinnamon. Big chunks of lamb melt into this delicious sauce.

So recently, some of the food looks like it could use more attention in the flavour department. Presentation seems sloppy too when the only decorations are the drips down the sides of the bowls and ceramic pots.

If you go to the Pegasus then, go for the fun of it. But don't expect impeccable things from the kitchen.

SANTORINI

1502 - Centre Street N. 276-8363

Sun, 4pm - 11pm; Tues-Thurs, 11am - 11pm; Fri, 11am - midnight; Sat, noon - midnight. Reservations recommended. Fully licensed. Non-smoking section. V, M, AE, DC. Summer outdoor dining. Belly dancer Fri & Sat evenings. Moderate.

People are amazingly faithful and intense about their favourite Greek restaurants. Mine is Santorini, my fave practically since it opened.

Partly it's my number one choice because of its look, a tri-level, blue and white place with plants and pictures of the Greek islands. A Greek restaurant that looks new somehow doesn't look authentic. The traffic of the years has added a patina of experience that Santorini wears well. The tiles on the main floor have darkened, the wood rails have yellowed a bit, and everything feels comfortable and settled.

It's also my choice because of the attitude. The owner feels that to maintain excellence and consistency, he must commit to being there most of the time. He and his staff are almost always on top of things, feeding the odd free ouzo to regulars and welcoming newcomers to the mysteries of mezethes and moussaka.

The food is my third reason for declaring Santorini as my favourite Greek restaurant. Spicy Greek meatballs, garlicky prawns, flaming kefalograviera cheese that doesn't go stringy. Buns spiced with cinnamon, nutmeg, and other secrets, beef souvlaki heavy with herbs and lemon, salads pungent with feta cheese, and arni kleftiko — the house lamb that dissolves in your mouth. It's rich, filling, food-hangover fare.

The menu holds no surprises for Greek-food fans. It's just that everything is so well prepared. There's the usual selection of appetizers, from hummus to spanakopita to the lemony avgolemono soup. There's lamb, beef, chicken, or prawn souvlakis, and sometimes there's roast suckling pig. And there's always baklava. Prices are reasonable, with dinner for two in the $40 range.

Eating at Santorini is the only time I can bring myself to drink retsina, plentiful at $13 a bottle. A cup of the flavoured mud called Greek coffee seems to work after one of their meals too. Heck, even ouzo goes down better with the taste of their lamb souvlaki in my mouth.

HOTELS

BOULEVARD CAFE

133 - 9 Avenue S.W. (The Palliser) 262-1234

Eclectic. Sun-Sat, 6:30am - 10pm. Reservations
recommended. Fully licensed. Non-smoking section. V, M,
AE, ER, DC, JCB. Hotel lounge. Moderate.

The Palliser Hotel has three places to eat, the Boulevard Cafe being the middle-of-the-road eatery situated in the basement. It's a surprisingly bright and soothing place, its art-deco decor splashed with warm pastels. Booths and tables are separated by plant-covered walls and high arches. Light comes from globe fixtures and high, sidewalk-level windows. First impressions are soft, peaceful, and private — a good start for any restaurant.

Service is prompt and good, as it should be in this sort of place. Most people are not there for leisurely dining. They are on a tight schedule, so efficiency is important.

The Boulevard does a pretty good breakfast of the usuals like French toast and pancakes and the unusuals like venison sausage and chorizo. There are all sorts of eggs, a New York steak, corned beef hash, and cheese-filled crêpes. Lunch and dinner span the traditional and the trendy. A barbecued duck salad roll snuggles up to the Caesar salad, smoked chicken breast with roasted peppers and chevre cheese sits beside a burger and a vegetarian sandwich. Low calorie and low salt dishes like veal marinated in herbs and yogurt or steamed red snapper with leeks and shiitake mushrooms are available. The famous Palliser clam chowder and French bread are also served. And on Tuesdays from 5 p.m. to 9 p.m., the Boulevard holds their "Death by Chocolate." Over a dozen desserts, from chocolate fondue to Black Forest cake, are laid out. At $9.50 for this buffet alone or $6.50 with a meal, you can do yourself in on chocolate.

So the Boulevard covers a lot of bases and most often does a pretty good job. It's quick, it's convenient, and it's comfortable. Just what's needed in a good hotel.

Upstairs, The Oak Room offers a pleasant alternative with its

Continental breakfast, buffet lunch, and afternoon high tea. And for those into a serious Dine, there's The Rimrock Room.

THE OWL'S NEST

320 - 4 Avenue S.W. (The Westin Hotel) 267-2823

Continental. Sun, 5:30pm - 10:30pm; Mon-Sat, 5:30pm - 11pm; Mon-Fri, 11:30am - 2:30pm. Reservations preferred. Fully licensed. Non-smoking section. V, M, AE, ER, DC, JCB. Hotel lounge. Expensive.

Whenever the debate about who's the best chef in town pops up, one name gets more votes than others. It's hard to dispute Fred Zimmerman's credentials and stack of medals from the World Culinary Olympics. He's a skilled chef capable of providing a stunning meal for two or two-hundred. And fortunately for Calgarians, he's The Westin Hotel's Executive Chef. As such, he supervises the much-hallowed Owl's Nest.

It's incredible that after twenty-five years The Owl's Nest still rates as one of the classiest places to dine in our city. It's purple and plush and warm, the perfect place for that special occasion. The polished silver gleams under soft lights as portraits of owls stare sternly at the tables. The finely dressed room is filled with finely dressed patrons, and staff move noiselessly about — appearing when needed, invisible when not. It's popular because it's so reliable and methodically excellent. There are no unpleasant surprises, just an enveloping sense of comfort and elegance.

Chef Zimmerman is renowned for his improvisations on Continental cuisine. He constantly tries new combinations and off-beat ingredients, challenging tradition. Consider dinner dishes like rainbow trout with toasted peanuts in a Southern salsa or duck breast with olives, saskatoons, and polenta or beef tenderloin sautéed with oyster mushrooms, cranberries, and Canadian whiskey. Consider supplementary menus created with specific themes like Italian or Californian cuisine. And consider lunchtime selections of low calorie, low salt alternatives that don't sacrifice flavour. Like a steak and citrus salad for $9.95 or prawns and scallops sautéed with peppers and tomatoes for $13.50.

There may be a few equals to The Owl's Nest, but no one surpasses it. From the highly trained staff to the warm zabaglione, The Owl's Nest is exceptional.

There's another decent eating establishment in the Westin. The Terrace is a peaceful, casual dining room well-known for its casual comfort and excellent Sunday brunch buffet. Open daily from 6:30 a.m. to 10 p.m., they serve breakfast, lunch, and dinner in a quiet pastel setting. The Charles Dickens' buffet served in December is a stomach-warming tribute to traditional British and British-Canadian Christmas food. From the Melton Mowbry pie to the trifle, it's a fine meal.

Across the lobby is The Cruvinet Wine Bar, a comfortable lounge that serves wines by the glass. It's good for a quick taste or a leisurely afternoon of wine experimenting — there are at least a half dozen wines to sample at any given time.

All of the Westin establishments combine class with high levels of service and quality, in keeping with their status as Calgary's leading hotel.

THE RIMROCK ROOM

133 - 9 Avenue S.W. (The Palliser) 262-1234

Continental. Sun, 10:30am - 2pm; Mon-Sat, 6pm - 10pm; Mon-Fri, 11:30am - 2pm. Reservations suggested. Fully licensed. Non-smoking section. V, M, AE, ER, DC, JCB. Hotel lounge. Sun buffet brunch. Pianist & dancing nightly. Expensive.

One of the oldest and most time-honoured dining rooms in town is The Rimrock Room in The Palliser Hotel. Almost anyone who's anyone who's passed through Calgary has at one time dined at the Rimrock or slept at The Palliser.

It's a classic hotel dining room done in Canadian Pacific style. At the east end of the hotel's recently renovated main floor, it's a large rectangular room split in half, with one side for smokers, the other for non-smokers. The south wall is covered with a thirty-eight foot long Western mural painted by Banff artist Charlie Beil in the early '60s. The west wall is brightened by a huge fireplace, and the high, arched ceiling is supported by teak pillars. These pillars are covered with hand-carved leather panels, completing the Western look. Tables are well spaced throughout the room, covered in white linens, and surrounded by cushy, high-backed chairs. It's worth a visit as much for the history as for the food.

Lunch at the Rimrock is an exercise in efficiency. Customers are met crisply at the door, coats swept away to the cloakroom. They're then breezed to their table and immediately presented with menus. Orders are taken, and the food arrives promptly. It's never pushy or rushed. It's a slick, professional approach tailored to downtown lunchers.

One of The Palliser's two most famous edibles is their clam chowder. It's a soup I've had many times, pleasantly smooth and light flavoured but sometimes too thick. I thought I'd be different, so I ordered their creamed chicken soup with almonds to start this particular lunch. A little starchy, but there was lots of chicken and almonds. It came with The Palliser's other famous product, the French bread which is baked in their brick oven. It was very soft inside yet crusty outside, and I'm told by Palliser regulars that it's been just as good for decades.

I followed my appetizer with the beef stroganoff special — a good-sized serving of tender beef in a thick gravy that suffered from heavy salting. It arrived with pasta and rice and slices of parsnips — a faux pas with the double starch, another faux pas with the plate presentation. Three off-white items on a plate are a definite no-no. Only a single sprig of broccoli added a little colour.

My partner's linguine with seafood was excellent. The pasta was light and fresh, and we wondered if anyone else had ordered it because it looked like they'd dropped all their seafood onto her plate. In a cream sauce, it was loaded with mussels, shrimp, prawns, lobster, and even some salmon. It was one of those times when I wanted to abandon my meal and delve into the other one.

The Rimrock offers desserts from one of those rolling trolleys. It's easy to refuse dessert from a menu, but much harder when it's wheeled under your nose. So I went for apple pie in a warm brandy sauce. Very nice.

The Rimrock has definitely kept up with current food trends. The dinner menu offers things like prawns and sweetbreads with cilantro and sun-dried tomatoes, smoked goose with a papaya coulis, and lobster, scallops, and prawns in a ginger-sake sauce. The chef hails from Switzerland via Vancouver, so future menus will reflect fare of the Pacific Northwest.

It's unfortunate that the coffee tastes like it's been drained off one of the trains. Otherwise, The Rimrock Room is a pleasant and elegant place to eat.

ITALIAN

BUON GIORNO

823 - 17 Avenue S.W. 244-5522

Sun, 2pm - 10pm; Mon-Thurs, 11am - 11pm; Fri & Sat, 11am - midnight. Reservations recommended. Fully licensed. Non-smoking section. V, M, AE, ER, DC. Moderate.

It looks as if the old Prairie Dog Inn, or PDI to regulars, has bitten the dust again. The former Mexican restaurant of choice for ages went strictly Italian about two years ago and seems to have no inclination to return to its southern roots. This place has gone through more name changes over the last two decades than I can count, but it always had that beer and all-you-can-eat burrito atmosphere.

What we have now is a fresh, clean, bright Italian diner, or trattoria, called Buon Giorno. The owners remain the same, and they've really put an effort into upgrading the old place to fit the upscaled tone of 17th Avenue. But the best thing about Buon Giorno is that it's not the least bit pretentious. Professional, yes. Pompous, no. Maybe that's a carryover from the old PDI days.

They've painted and cleaned and acquired new tables that you can't carve your initials into anymore. There are real tablecloths (the red and white checked variety) with blue napkins. And there's an air-conditioning system that can chill a glass of water in seconds. They do keep it cool in there.

I think of Buon Giorno as an Italian diner, not only because of the look but because of the menu. It's straightforward, the same style that lots of other places pawn off as something much grander. There are pastas, veals, chicken, the usual antipastos, and soups. The top dish of pasta (all made in-house) runs in at $9.95. Veal dishes top out at $12.95. Healthy-sized lunch specials are mostly in the $6 to $8 range. All dishes are served with the generic Italian rolls heated to within an inch of their lives. In general, it's fair quality for the price. It's not award-winning food, but it's good, fresh, and aplenty.

We tried a few different things on our lunch visit, from a veal sandwich to mussels in a creamy basil sauce to the veal Amalfitana, and all were okay. The sandwich was the best of the works — a nice piece of grilled veal with cheese, lettuce, and a searing hot pepper. My Italian friend said that it tasted as authentic as any he'd had. Served with a bowl of straciatelle soup — that's chicken broth with whipped egg — it made a nice midday meal. The mussels were also quite good, done very simply in a sauce that was more milky than creamy. The vitello Amalfitana was the most expensive plate we ordered, but at $12.95, it was worth the price in volume alone. Three big slices of veal (not the greatest cut, but tender enough to cut with a fork) were topped with cheese, artichoke hearts, and a mustard sauce. It would have been better had the artichokes not tasted so funny (they were too sour for some reason). Served with a side dish of linguine in meat sauce, there were no bells and whistles, but it was better than average.

On another visit, the spaghetti carbonara was excellent. A very simple dish of bacon, cheese, and egg on pasta, it was well seasoned and textured.

In general, although I'm sad to see the demise of the PDI, I'm quite happy with Buon Giorno. If I went there for a top-end Italian meal, I might be disappointed. But as a friendly Italian trattoria, it works.

CHIANTI

1438 - 17 Avenue S.W. 229-1600

Sun, 4pm - midnight; Mon-Sat, 11am - midnight.
Reservations recommended. Fully licensed. Non-smoking
section. V, M, AE, ER. Take-out. Summer outdoor dining.
Cheap-moderate.

It doesn't seem possible that Chianti can hold 128 people. I'm sure that when it first opened it only sat thirty or forty. But it keeps expanding, and more and more tables are shoehorned in. They've opened eateries in Edmonton and Vancouver too and have two local sister restaurants, Fiore and Toscano. But as the cornerstone of the Chianti empire, the original Chianti Café and Restaurant is still the best of the clan.

Chianti's calling card is good, cheap, fast Italian food. It's simply, but thoughtfully, prepared — things like fettuccine in butter and black pepper or veal in a lemon sauce. You'll probably do a double take at the prices: spaghetti alla Bolognese for $4.75, veal-filled ravioli for $5.25, half orders of pasta for $3.50. Lunch for ten bucks, including a reasonable tip, is easy. And you'll have time left over to browse along 17th Avenue before heading back to work.

With twenty pastas, fifteen veals, a raft of appetizers and house specials, and a blackboard crammed with daily offerings, you should be able to find something to eat. On my most recent visit, I skipped the pastas and started with the daily soup instead. A vegetable-based minestrone, it had a flavourful broth and plenty of clams. A fine start to the meal. I followed that with the pollo arrosto, a favourite of many Chianti regulars. This is a roasted half chicken coated in a demi-glace sauce and served with big chunks of roasted carrots, zucchini, and potato. Too much really for lunch, it's a straightforward dish that works.

My partner's mixed salad seemed to include everything green that was in the kitchen, but the dressing was too tart with vinegar. His combo pasta plate of fettuccine in a creamy meat sauce and pesto ravioli was good. He felt the creamy basil sauce was more successful than the meat one though.

Effective service and a well-defined non-smoking section help you forget that Chianti is very busy and very crowded. But if you want to get into the Chianti mood, you might try a litre of their specially labeled Italian wine (a quite palatable red Merlot or a white Gambellara) for $13.75, possibly the best vino deal in town.

CLAUDIO'S TRATTORIA

355 - 10 Avenue S.W. 234-0990

Mon-Fri, 11:30am - midnight; Sat & Sun, 5pm - midnight. Reservations recommended. Fully licensed. Non-smoking section. V, M, AE. Lounge. Take-out. Moderate.

Usually I visit a restaurant once or twice for a radio review. Occasionally I make three trips simply because I like a place. Besides, you can't do too much research. Anyway, that's just what I did at Claudio's. Lots of research.

Claudio's may ring a familiar bell because a pretty good restaurant of the same name used to reside on 11th Avenue. The LaMonaca brothers, those well-known proprietors of Electric Avenue fame, operated it. But when the young singles crowd overran the strip, restaurant patrons thinned out and Claudio's shut down. Now, after almost two years in hiatus, Claudio's has reopened at the corner of 10th Avenue and 4th Street S.W., a great location that has never done well. But Claudio's concept is stunning, and it's sure to grab a Calgarian or two.

The interior is part Greco-Roman ruin, part New Mexican garage sale. Plastered walls are stripped away in spots to reveal bricks, long trailing drapes cover full-length windows, and huge wooden chandeliers dangle over Arizona-coloured booths. Trees sprout right out of the floor, and ancient-looking beams support the ceiling. It's fun, casual, and active enough to keep your eyes busy.

But the bill of fare will snatch your attention quickly. It's the most innovative Italian menu in Calgary. Drawing on various regions of Italy, it's a rustic cuisine that looks like it wandered through Southern California before stopping here. A soup of wild mushrooms and artichokes. Tuna carpaccio with a grainy mustard mayonnaise. Veal chops with porcini mushrooms in a Barolo sauce. Dynamite stuff.

On my last visit my partner tried a salad of bocconcini cheese, tomato, and fresh basil in vinaigrette. A beautiful, fresh summer plate with good cheese, perfect basil, and as is so often the case unless you grow your own, okay tomatoes. I opted for a creamy smoked-chicken soup with a light tomatoey flavour. For our main courses, we ordered the pizza quattro stagione and some bucatini pasta. The pizza, done on a thin but bready crust, was divided into four different sections: basil and tomato, porcini and onion, artichoke hearts and fontina cheese, and sausage and tomato sauce. Just terrific. And the bucatini with porcini, sausage, and pecorino cheese was spicy yet balanced and loaded with flavour.

But our meals weren't the only good things. Three bottles sit on each table: one filled with extra virgin olive oil; another with virgin olive oil, a chili, rosemary, and garlic; and yet another with balsamic vinegar. These can be drizzled on whatever you'd like, and the staff encourage you to pour the oils onto a plate so that you can dip their dense peasant loaf in it. This is a change from butter, a change at which I saw one customer turn up her nose. But give it a try. Fresh Italian bread and olive oil — a simple pleasure.

Desserts are wonderful. Like the rich mascarpone cheesecake or the waffle cup filled with fresh berries and zabaglione. The wine list is flexible and reasonably priced, just like the food menu. Pizzas range from $7 to $9 for the single-serving size, pastas range from $7 to $8, salads and antipastos from $4 to $7. And since the menu is updated monthly to reflect seasonal produce, you won't be easily bored.

I could go on at length, but I'd rather go to Claudio's. Italian food in Calgary took a major step forward when it opened.

DA GUIDO

2001 - Centre Street N. 276-1365

Mon-Sat, 5pm - midnight; Mon-Fri, 11:30am - 3pm.
Reservations recommended. Fully licensed. Non-smoking
section. V, M, AE, ER, DC. Moderate-expensive.

When I give a bad review, I usually return sometime later to give the place a second chance. In my ten years of reviewing, I've only modified my opinion two or three times. And this is one such occasion.

A while back I had a terrible evening at Da Guido. Service was appalling, the room was cramped and smoky, the menu was boring, and the food was so-so. And I said as much on the radio. Afterwards the owner called me to express his concern and to ask me specifically what the problems had been. I told him that the service had been appalling, the room cramped and smoky, the menu boring, and the food so-so. He told me that he had fired the waiter (yikes!), was building a new restaurant, and was revamping his menu. In September 1990, Da Guido reopened in a new location with better service, a spacious room, and a subtly unique menu. From the bocconcini cheese stuffed with anchovies to the Italian sausage with polenta, you'll find many dishes that appear nowhere else in town.

I love risotto, a not-so-simple Italian rice dish. Until my visit to the new Da Guido, I'd never had it prepared properly in Calgary. It should be done with arborio rice (a short, fat grain) that has been cooked to a delicate, creamy texture. Guido's dinner menu offers six variations of it. The one I tried as an appetizer had been simmered in a stock with wild mushrooms and topped with parmesan. It was perfect. And a bowl of spaghetti gorgonzola brought the smooth blue cheese taste to the pasta without inundating it. The flavour built with each forkful. A wonderful start to our meal.

The veal saltimbocca — a very Roman dish of veal, prosciutto, and sage — was pungent with the taste of fresh sage. The osso bucco was excellent in its traditional red wine and tomato sauce. Draped over saffron rice, the contrast between the red and yellow colours was attractive. Even our vegetables — carrots, potato, and broccoli — were done to a turn. With a shared dessert of the layered biscuit and mascarpone cheese concoction known as tiramisu and a bottle of excellent house wine for $16, we were stuffed.

The new Da Guido is a pretty place. A large foyer splits it into two rooms, each seating about forty. Fireplaces, offset lighting, and high-backed chairs bring an elegance to the restaurant. It's a reasonably serious place to dine where you'll feel more comfortable if you're dressed up a bit. But it's not stuffy, providing a livelier alternative to the subdued tones of some other fancy places. Service is ingratiating, at times a little too much so, and more attention is occasionally paid to some customers than to others. But in general, it's professional and slick. (I should note that on this visit the maître d' recognized me, so we were two of the "favoured" ones.)

Da Guido has the best wine list of any Italian restaurant in Calgary. They've imported dozens of wines directly from Italy, wines that are largely unavailable elsewhere.

It appears that a lot of thought and concern have gone into the redevelopment of Da Guido. I'm happy to say that it bears little resemblance to the place I panned. Salut!

FIORE CANTINA

638 - 17 Avenue S.W. 244-6603

Sun, 4pm - 11pm; Mon-Thurs, 11am - 11pm; Fri & Sat, 11am - 11:30pm. Reservations recommended. Fully licensed. Non-smoking section. V, M, AE, ER, DC. Take-out. Summer outdoor dining. Cheap-moderate.

Located on 17th Avenue in a space previously inhabited by a couple of unlucky restaurants, Fiore exudes a comfortable Italian trattoria feel. It's run by the people from Chianti Café and Restaurant down the street. Chianti has been popular ever since it opened because it serves decent food at great prices, and this tradition has been carried on at Fiore.

But Fiore is a little less manic with its calm green and beige decor and its planters. Some of the tables are even spaced comfortably apart. The south and west walls are all glass, so the place is warmed by natural light. It's divided into three sections with the poorest area given over to non-smoking, but it's still a relaxing place to unwind.

They've gone beyond the norm of local Italian food. Not much, but it's noticeable. All the old standards are there, but they've included pasta with hot peppers or asparagus and cream cheese and veal with hearts of palm or mustard-wine sauce or gorgonzola. Not one dish costs over $10.

I've had an appetizer of figs and prosciutto where the ham had been thickly cut (with the fat trimmed off) and then wrapped around the figs. It was a sweet, meaty dish. A nice change from the usual melon and prosciutto. And I was amazed by the amount of meat — a huge portion for only $4.75.

I've also tried an outstanding chicken and spinach soup — a clear broth seasoned with nutmeg and filled with juicy chunks of chicken. It was followed by a combination pasta plate of spinach fettuccine with salmon and capers and ricotta-stuffed ravioli in tomato sauce. The red sauce, green noodles, and pink fish made for an attractive presentation. As a daily special with the soup, my meal amounted to $8.95. Hard to beat. Especially with a bottle of Chianti Brolio as a daily special at $13.95.

But Fiore is not perfect. It's capable of mediocrity as well as excellence. A lunch of mushroom soup and risotto was lackluster. The soup tasted bland, and the risotto wasn't really risotto at all. In any true risotto I've had, arborio rice has been cooked in stock and ends up almost creamy. In an attempt at economy I suppose, my risotto at Fiore was just regular steamed rice topped with a seafood and tomato sauce. Not bad in its own way, but not risotto. I'm told, however, that since my lunch, it's being prepared in the proper fashion. I'll have to venture back soon to see if the rumours are true.

GALLO'S

815A - 49 Avenue S.W.
(Britannia Shopping Plaza) 243-9307

*Mon-Sat, 11am - 9pm. Reservations preferred. Fully
licensed. Non-smoking section. V, M. Moderate.*

Fans of PizzaMaria will remember the smiling face of Maria waltzing
out wonderful pizzas in the little Bridgeland eatery. The pizza there is
still excellent, but Maria and husband Pat have moved on, opening a new
restaurant in the old Edelweiss location.

This time they've christened their restaurant with their last name
instead of Maria's first. They've cleaned and brightened the place into a
pleasant, cheery room with three distinct areas. It's cozy and charming
with big north windows drawing in light during the day.

Pat makes possibly the best pizza in town. Whether you try the
"normal" pizzas, like Hawaiian on a thick crust, or their Calabrese-style
ones on thin crusts, the dough is excellent and perfectly cooked right on
the bricks of Pat's oven. Pizzas such as the quattro formaggi with four
cheeses or the di amore with red peppers, pesto, and artichoke hearts
provide interesting eating. Many of the ingredients — the sautéed
peppers, the pesto, the pickled eggplant — are prepared in-house.

Gallo's new menu has moved upscale though, with the addition of
more pastas, veals, and chicken dishes. Everything is fresh and authentic
in a strong, southern Italian, home-cooked way. The fettuccine con
funghi features huge chunks of mushrooms in a rich tomato-cream sauce.
The pollo pesto bathes a boneless chicken breast in a balanced, lime-
green pesto cream. Surrounded by tomato-sauced rotini, it makes for a
pretty, full-flavoured meal. Even their simple stuffed eggplant is good
enough to make me ask for seconds, and this is one of my least favourite
vegetables.

Gallo's offers an imaginative wine list, almost all Italian vino
(including Italian dessert wine). But for those wanting a non-alcoholic
pick-me-up, a Crodo limone drink is almost as good.

So whether it's pizza or pasta fagiole, Gallo's is the best place for
good Calabrese cooking and hospitality.

LA PASTA

320 - 16 Avenue N.W. 276-8184

Mon-Sat, 5pm - 11pm; Wed-Fri, 11:30am - 2pm.
Reservations recommended. Fully licensed. Non-smoking
section. V, M, AE, ER. Moderate.

La Pasta is housed along with Mamma's Ristorante in a big white building on 16th Avenue N.W. They share the same kitchen, but Mamma's (not to be confused with Mamma's Pizzeria next door) is a more formal room than La Pasta. A little austere on the outside, La Pasta is one of Calgary's prettiest Italian restaurants inside. With its open courtyard look, it's huge. Yet it breaks nicely into private nooks and crannies, allowing a reasonable set up for smokers and non-smokers.

After all the years that they've been open, this is still one busy place. La Pasta bustles and hums with activity. And yet the level of service has always been high. Professional, yet personable, effective, and attentive. No faults here.

Waiters prepare the evening antipasto plates from huge trays laid out as a centerpiece for the room, and they always do an admirable job. The selection is extensive, from cold meats and pickled vegetables to cheeses and olives. All high quality. Probably the best traditional Italian antipasto in town. Another decent way to start your meal is with their tomato and onion salad.

It wouldn't be right to go to La Pasta and not order pasta, so that's what I always do. On my last visit, I tried the fusilli smothered in mushrooms, pancetta, and onion. The pasta, a mixture of spinach, carrot, and egg noodles, blended prettily on the plate under a creamy tomato sauce. Touched by the smokiness of the pancetta, it was a terrific dish, but almost too much to finish.

La Pasta's kitchen is very accommodating, willing to prepare items not on the menu if they can. We failed, however, in our search for a simple dish of linguine with fresh basil. I find it a little surprising for a good Italian restaurant to not have fresh basil in mid-July. Anyway, my companion's second choice of chicken in pesto sauce was more than adequate. Tons of this basil and garlic sauce swamped the tender chicken breast.

The lunch and dinner menus are quite similar, with a selection of pastas as well as seafood, veal, and chicken dishes. Prices skyrocket for the evening fare though. I don't know how much more or less you are served, but I'm sure it couldn't account for the fillet of sole in lemon sauce being $8.95 at lunch and then $17.95 at dinner. Granted the dinner menu says that it's on a slice of eggplant, but how much does eggplant cost these days? A half dozen Italian-style escargots on the lunch menu is $3.95. A half dozen on the dinner menu is $6.95. Intriguing.

They offer a typical selection of Italian desserts like zabaglione, spumoni ice cream, and tiramisu, as well as an adequate Italian wine list.

Evening prices aside, La Pasta remains a strong alternative for those searching out a good old Italian meal.

LA PICCOLA NAPOLI

Macleod Trail & Lake Fraser Gate S.E.
(Avenida Bonavista Shopping Centre) 278-2282

Mon-Sat, 5pm - 11pm; Wed-Fri, 11:30am - 2pm.
Reservations required. Fully licensed. Non-smoking
section. V, M, AE. Moderate-expensive.

Look way down south on Macleod Trail, almost to Midnapore, and you'll see a new shopping centre called Avenida Bonavista. It has a different look and a different attitude. The look is Spanish with fountains, pastel plaster walls, and ceramic tile roofs. The attitude is tony with small, high quality operations. And they've managed to attract some decent eateries, including La Piccola Napoli Ristorante.

La Piccola Napoli was transplanted from Willow Park Village where it was known as La Piccola Italia. The new restaurant has rooted itself in a larger space and has been over-decorated to a point that actually works. Multiple levels with railings, brass and brick, and pillars and plants give it an outdoorsy, Italian-terrace feel. It's an approach that creates pockets of privacy and comfort for diners. Professional waiters whirl about, but they aren't just passing through. These guys are serious — crisp and sharp and helpful.

Over the last few years I've been complaining about mediocre Italian look-alikes with sticky fettuccine Alfredos and excessively garlicked Caesars. Now the menu at La Piccola Napoli is far from startling, but they do what they do very well. There's nothing wrong with an Alfredo if it's done right.

La Piccola Napoli starts off dinner with eight appetizers, from a plate of mixed Italian meats or prosciutto with melon to mussels or jumbo shrimp. I've sampled the latter, bubbling away in butter and garlic; they're good, but pricy at $9.75 for only six crustaceans.

More reasonable are the pastas, with the most expensive dinner version priced at $10.50. The fettuccine alla Valentino with pancetta, peas, cream, and tomato sauce tastes great. Freshly made pasta is cooked until al dente and coated in a thick, creamy sauce with loads of bacon and peas.

They offer a number of veal dishes, from the simple style stuffed with prosciutto to the delicate and deliciously sweet scaloppine with mushrooms, cream, and apricot brandy. I've tried a daily special of osso bucco, braised veal shank in a thick, tomatoey red wine sauce, and it was excellent. A minor disappointment was the lack of the traditional marrow-filled bone, the marrow being considered a delicacy by many

70

(hence the name osso bucco, which translates as bone with a hole). Apparently they usually do serve the bone, but there had been a mix up at the supplier's end. With a pile of mixed vegetables on the side, this was a big meal.

Overall, La Piccola Napoli is a good new restaurant in a great new location. And the fountain outside is an elegant Mediterranean touch.

TRATTORIA D'ITALIA

302 - Crowchild Trail N.W. 283-3331

Sun, 5pm - 10pm (closed Sun in July & August); Mon-Sat, 5pm - 11pm; Mon-Fri, 11:30am - 2pm. Reservations recommended, especially on weekends. Fully licensed. Non-smoking section. V, M, AE. Moderate.

The Trattoria D'Italia began as an out-of-the-way pizzeria with pictures of the Italian World Cup soccer champions, a couple of foosball tables, washroom doors that didn't close right, killer espresso, and great pizzas. They renovated a few times and finally moved to another location on Crowchild Trail. It's easy to reach if you're heading north, but heaven help you if you're heading south.

All the old fun stuff has disappeared, including the pizzas (except as an occasional luncheon special). Instead, the new Trattoria D'Italia offers some of the better classical Italian preparations in town. Even though more contemporary styles of Italian cooking are making the scene, it's still good to have some of the old standards around.

I've always liked the Caesar salad at the Trattoria D'Italia. It's genuinely mouth-puckering with lemon and anchovies and reeks of parmesan and garlic (you will too). Nicely balanced, it's worth every mouthful. The pastas are always good — well sauced and never gummy. The fettuccine Gigi with ham, mushrooms, green pepper, onion, and olives in a creamy tomato sauce is comforting. A thick (but not gluey) sauce coats the beautiful, freshly made noodles. This sauce is equaled by the mushroom sauce on the veal scaloppine. But when the owner is also the chef, you have a better chance of receiving a quality meal. Desserts of zabaglione and tiramisu add to the classic charm of the place. There are no surprises here, just a strong, expert approach to a fine cuisine.

JAPANESE

SUKIYAKI HOUSE

517 - 10 Avenue S.W. 262-9153

Sun, 5pm - 10pm; Mon-Thurs, 5pm - 11pm; Fri & Sat, 5pm - midnight; Mon-Fri, 11:30am - 2pm. Reservations preferred. Fully licensed. Non-smoking section. V, M, AE, DC, JCB. Take-out. Moderate.

Japanese restaurants always seem to be popular with the business crowd. Aside from the opportunity to act like a corporate shogun on an expense account, they provide a clean, light meal in calm surroundings. I think that's why the Sukiyaki House on 10th Avenue has continued to be popular after fifteen years.

They have used their location well, creating a quiet garden setting on the edge of our humming downtown core. Most basement restaurants have the dark, dingy look of a dungeon, but not the Sukiyaki House. Down a set of stairs, you cross a small bridge over a trickling pond and enter the restaurant. The transition from corporate to pastoral is emphatic. It is impossible to carry all your business headaches over that bridge.

Like many Japanese restaurants, the Sukiyaki House is broken into sections: the shoeless *tatami* rooms, a separate sushi-bar room, and an open space with tables scattered about. Screens and decorative windows divide areas, creating quiet alcoves and small party spots. It should be possible to find a space to fit your mood.

We sat at a table in the smokeless sushi-bar room, the perfect chance to watch the sushi chefs at work. Slick they are, slicing the fish, wadding the rice, dabbing the wasabi — a true study in concentration. Between preparations, they chat energetically with customers, but while performing their tasks, they are a lesson in stoicism.

Their sushi is always very good, so we tried some as an appetizer along with some gyoza (pan-fried dumplings) and a small order of tempura. The gyoza, stuffed with ground beef and vegetables, were quite savoury, especially when dipped in the accompanying vinegared soya sauce. The tempura were light and crunchy, as they should be.

Our main courses of oyako donburi — or oyako don for short — and salmon teriyaki were likewise very good. The oyako don consisted of a big bowl of rice topped with onions and incredibly tender chicken in a sukiyaki sauce. Capped with beaten egg, it was a delicate preparation that brought out the flavour of each ingredient. Masterfully prepared. (Oyako means parent and child, a humorous reference to the chicken and egg.) The large salmon steak came coated with a thick, pungent teriyaki sauce, not exactly the least salty thing on the menu, but still very fresh and flavourful. It was as impressive as the first time I tasted it here a number of years ago. But I wish someone would invent salmon without bones. Although usually a fairly easy fish to eat, this one seemed to be reeking revenge by hiding more bones than a salmon should.

After all that food, reaching only the $30 mark, we weren't painfully full. Quite satisfied mind you, but no room for any green tea ice cream. That rice did seem to expand.

I'd like to note two things about the Sukiyaki House. The staff are always pleasant and courteous. Kimono-clad waitresses deftly deliver meals and smile as they softly clear tables. And the food itself is intricately crafted and decorated, Japanese-style, on ceramic plates and bowls, maintaining the beauty and symmetry of the fare.

It's comforting to know that a place that has been around so long is still as good as ever. There is another Sukiyaki House at 211 - Banff Avenue (762-2002) in Banff.

SUSHI HIRO

727 - 5 Avenue S.W. 233-0605

Mon-Sat, 5pm - 11pm; Mon-Fri, 11:30am - 2pm.
Reservations recommended on weekends. Fully licensed.
Non-smoking section. V, M, AE, ER, DC, JCB. Take-out.
Moderate.

Probably the liveliest of Calgary's Japanese eateries is Sushi Hiro Restaurant. As opposed to the quiet elegance of the Yuzuki and the Sukiyaki House, Sushi Hiro is bubbly and animated. The *itamaes,* or sushi chefs, welcome their regulars with loud greetings and large smiles as the crush of lunch bodies fills the single large room. Theirs is also a business-like approach to Japanese cuisine. Everything is done in a hurry at lunch, catering to the needs of the downtown office crowd.

The bow to efficiency detracts from some presentations. Many of the plates are plastic, and the food appears to have been hurried onto them. More attention seems to be paid at dinner, however, than lunch.

For the uninitiated, sushi's key ingredient is its specially prepared rice made with vinegar and sugar. This is combined in different ways with other ingredients like raw fish, omelette, or cucumber. To accommodate the lunch rush, much of Sushi Hiro's noon sushi is assembled before you order it — not a long time in advance, but enough to ensure that you won't have to wait for the preparation. I'm of two minds on this: Although I appreciate the fast service, I enjoy the tradition of watching my sushi in the making. And besides, if they are doing it ahead of time, it shouldn't be as sloppy as it sometimes turns out. I've received it with portions of tuna pieced together rather than one long slice of fish or with the rolls off-balance because of too much rice on one side. Nonetheless, it still tastes good.

At a recent lunch, I had the ton katsu, a breaded pork loin served with a thick, fruity sauce. The meat was simply fried so that it maintained its flavour, and the sauce suited the pork to a T. With a small salad and a bowl of rice, it made a more than adequate lunch, especially considering the $5.80 price-tag.

Sample some hot sake if you're bold. I'm told that it's the best companion to sushi and sashimi. Me, I'll stick to the green tea thanks.

YUZUKI JAPANESE RESTAURANT & SUSHI BAR

510 - 9 Avenue S.W. 261-7701

Sun, 5pm - 9pm; Tues-Sat, 5pm - 10pm; Mon-Fri, 11:30am - 2pm. Reservations preferred. Fully licensed. Non-smoking section. V, M, AE, DC. Lounge. Take-out. Moderate.

There used to be a little Japanese restaurant in Acadia Shopping Centre called the Yuzuki. It was difficult to find because the entrance was tucked obscurely along the side, and it wasn't adequately signed. The cinder block construction and lack of windows gave it a laundromat storage room look, yet it served the best Japanese food in Calgary.

It closed in 1985, but like the rising moon after which it was named, the Yuzuki has risen again. This time it's downtown in a space that is much larger, and it even has windows. In fact, for those who feel claustrophobic in Japanese restaurants with all the tiny booths and screens, the Yuzuki is very open. It's spread over two levels with a sushi bar at one end and some private booths, or *tatami* rooms, around the outside for people who like to dine shoeless.

They've created an Oriental atmosphere with kimonoed waitresses and Japanese music. It's all very relaxing, especially for a lunchtime escape from the business world. Sometimes, though, the staff are too relaxed — fifteen minutes is far too long to wait for a copy of the lunch menu.

The assorted sushi luncheon includes eleven or so pieces of sushi.

There are mounds of the vinegared rice topped with raw or cooked or marinated seafood. There are seaweed wrapped rolls of the rice filled with cucumber, sea leg, omelette, and dried gourd. And there are deep-fried tofu pouches stuffed with a sushi-rice mixture. All for only $6.50, it is an exceptional price.

Their tempura is just as it should be: A light, crispy casing coats seafood and various vegetables. It's always fresh, with the vegetables still crunchy and the seafood still firm. Their gyoza, savoury Japanese dumplings, are denser and smaller than their Peking counterparts, but very similar otherwise. Both the beef and the chicken teriyaki are tender and tasty, although the chicken sometimes suffers from too much fat, a problem that the otherwise good yakitori (chicken kabobs) has occasionally as well.

I don't go to Japanese restaurants expecting lots of food. I expect delicate preparation and beautiful presentation to go along with freshness. It's a pleasant surprise to find quantity as well as quality at the Yuzuki. Perhaps some presentations suffer because the plates are so full. Still, the sushi line up and curve around the wooden serving trays while carved radishes hold the pungent green horseradish, wasabi. Tempura shrimp form teepees with their tails pointing skyward on bamboo plates. The gyoza dough is sealed with an intricate series of pleats.

The lunch menu offers a good overview of Japanese fare with its sushi and sashimi, tempura and teriyaki, soups and sukiyaki, and the dinner menu takes things even further with things like cold noodle salads and those full-meal deals called donburis. Not everyone is longing for octopus sushi.

The Yuzuki has been away for years, but now that it's back, it's still the best.

LATIN AMERICAN

BLUE HOUSE CAFE

3843 - 19 Street N.W. 284-9111

Latin American. Tues-Sun, 5pm - 11pm. Reservations
recommended, especially for Fri & Sat. Fully licensed.
Non-smoking section. V, M, AE. Moderate.

I'm always searching for new restaurants with new cuisines, and I'm always happy to find a good one. Like the Blue House Cafe, the only place in Calgary serving a selection of Latin American fare. We don't tend to see much food from south of Mexico, so it's a refreshing change.

The Blue House hasn't been around that long, and consequently, it's still quite unknown. Just off Northmount Drive at 19th Street N.W., it's not exactly in a major restaurant district either. And it looks like a quiet neighborhood pub or pizza parlour from the outside.

The Blue House started out cautiously: The owner is Colombian, and he wasn't sure how well his food would sell. So, he kept some of the popular dishes from the Central European restaurant that was formerly located here and included some Latin American-style food that he thought Calgarians would like. But the schnitzels and the Bavarian sausages are gone now, opening up space for more Latin American dishes.

The menu offers things like paella or shrimp in a cilantro sauce or ceviche (citrus-marinated seafood) or a Nicaraguan beef dish cooked with tomatoes, onions, and green peppers. There's a real Spanish tone to the food with its use of hot weather herbs, peppers, and lots of beef and seafood.

No distinctly Latin American soups were available the day we visited, so we started our dinner with an impressive rendition of cream of mushroom and an alphabet soup with loads of noodle letters in chicken broth. Flavoured with cilantro, the alphabet soup took us a bit south of the border.

From there we traveled all the way with the Colombian churrasco, a broiled sirloin steak marinated in Colombian seasonings that the chef keeps secret. Just great. Often steak is lost under so much salty seasoning or goopy barbecue sauce that you could be eating cardboard and not know it. This meat, cut thin, was tender and full of natural flavour. A warning though: You may look at it and think that since it's only a half inch thick, it's not much of a steak. But it really is good, just a little small like some of their other servings.

We also enjoyed an unusual dish of red snapper baked in a cherry sauce — not exactly the national dish of Colombia, but created by a Colombian chef so close enough for me. The snapper picked up the cherry flavour in tasty juxtaposition to some onion. There's other seafood cooked with fruit sauces too — scampi sautéed in a creamy papaya sauce, for instance, or a mixture of shellfish in a pineapple sauce — showing once and for all that California cuisine doesn't hold a monopoly on interesting combinations.

For dessert we had a smooth almond pudding and a carrot cake that looked suspiciously like my mother's, but had too much dried fruit and was a tad dry. Colombian coffee is on tap as well as Spanish and Chilean wines, among a few others.

The Blue House is comfortable, seating about forty patrons in two sections. It comes as no surprise that the decor is predominantly blue — blue curtains, blue napkins, even blue flowers — all offset by clean white walls and tablecloths. And this place has the shiniest glasses and cutlery around. It's an exceptionally clean restaurant. I don't often notice a restaurant because of its cleanliness, but here, I did.

The staff create a casual atmosphere and take the time to talk to their customers while still giving good service.

JUAN'S

807 - 1 Street S.W. 266-0051

Mexican. Mon, 11am - 9pm; Tues-Fri, 11am - 10pm; Sat, noon - 10pm. Reservations not accepted. Fully licensed. No non-smoking section. V, M, AE. Moderate.

I mentioned Juan's to someone who works less than a block away from its 1st Street location. In spite of her interest in trying new places, she had never heard of it. That's the trouble with being a tiny, out-of-the-way hole-in-the-wall. A lot of people never notice you.

But enough people have noticed Juan's. Lunchers hover near the door, waiting to snag the next table that comes free. And for any fan of real Mexican food, the wait is worth it. Mexican cuisine, when done properly, ranks among the world's great cuisines, like French and Chinese.

Juan himself used to be involved with the Salt & Pepper, but broke off to start his own place. It's great to see a situation where both the original and the splinter group have managed to maintain high standards. As a personal preference, I lean towards Juan's because of the way he brings out the intense Mexican flavours.

A green mole sauce may not sound particularly appetizing — and it didn't look that great either — but this creamy sauce of green peppers, green onions, and green herbs packed a velvety wallop. Poured over chicken and rice, it created the robust pollo con mole verdhe. With a small tossed salad and some refried beans that actually tasted like beans instead of wallpaper paste, this was a fine lunch. I preceeded it with Juan's daily soup, a lentil concoction. Sounds as boring as lima beans right? No way. It was dynamite. Thick, creamy, not at all starchy. Sizzling in the mouth, yet soothing at the same time.

The rest of the menu has little resemblance to the quick and dirty Sorta-Mex places around. The words "enchilada" and "burrito" pop up, but not in the typical north-of-the-border parlance with cutesy descriptions. The enchiladas de pollo con mole is a dish of chicken-stuffed tortillas with a mole poblano, a sauce deepened with roasted chili peppers and bitter chocolate — the dark sister of the mole verdhe. The ensalada de aguacate is an avocado salad with a Thai-like lime dressing. There's halibut in white wine and tomato sauce or shrimp in garlic and chili peppers. Be careful of the huevos con chorizo, translated as scrambled eggs with Mexican sausages. Sounds like breakfast, but only if you like it spicy — these are not the harmless little pork sausages you'll find at truck stops. Juan offers several desserts too, the most notable being the crepas con cajeta, crêpes filled with a densely sweet goat milk syrup.

I also like Juan's because you can't get lost in there. It's so small you can almost serve yourself. Except that they are one step ahead of you, replenishing the ice water from a tall frosted glass pitcher. And if you're in a hurry, your courses arrive practically on top of each other. But if you're into a more leisurely evening, there's a big cooler of Corona behind the counter. Or one of Juan's coffees with tequila, Kahlua, brandy, and cinnamon.

SALT & PEPPER

4351 - Macleod Trail S. 243-3173

Mexican. Sun, noon - 9:30pm; Mon-Fri, 11am - 11pm; Sat, 4pm - 11pm. Reservations not accepted. Fully licensed. No non-smoking section. V, M, AE, DC. Take-out. Summer outdoor dining. Sun à la carte brunch. Cheap-moderate.

Somehow Calgary missed out on landing any good Mexican restaurants until a few years ago. Then the Salt & Pepper opened up on Macleod Trail. Now that's not a typical Mexican name, but it was the name of the original restaurant in this spot. When the current owners bought the place and changed it to a Mexican eatery, they decided to keep the name. After all, Mexican food does use lots of peppers.

Thirty-odd seats are squeezed into a tiny room in the corner of an automotive mall. There are a few Mexican mementos here and there, and two walls of windows offer a great view of Macleod Trail. It's not all that comfortable — it sort of feels like a place for a quick coffee. And sometimes the service suffers from too many customers and not enough staff. But the people are friendly enough to make the whole experience more appealing. They're helpful and very knowledgeable, and they tell a mean joke. This is no fly-by-night operation.

The food is quite good. They make their own chorizo, a coarsely ground, peppery sausage that they serve fried and topped with melted mozzarella. It's not a real flaming chorizo, but it's spicy enough to make you sit up and take notice. The Salt & Pepper's Mexican food is like that. It's not Tex-Mex or Cal-Mex. It's authentic Mex. They use recipes from Tampico and Veracruz and Mazatlan. It's an eclectic "best of" Mexican menu that will look unfamiliar to those who frequent Chi-Chi's. Oh there are tacos and tortilla chips, but there's also red snapper in Creole sauce and marinated whitefish. On Sundays, in addition to their regular menu, you can order things like huevos rancheros or huevos con chorizo off their brunch menu.

I've had their pork chops with adobo sauce, a tangy, tomatoey creation almost like my barbecue sauce. An excellent taste, but I wish they had used thick chops instead of those skinny little quarter-inch ones. Their enchiladas de pollo con mole are stuffed with shredded chicken and smothered in a great mole sauce made with five different kinds of dried peppers, peanuts, and dark chocolate. Now that's distinctive. It's dark brown, with a smooth, deep bite. It would be better, however, with more chicken inside those tortillas.

On my last visit, I had butterflied sirloin, Tampico-style. Simply grilled with mild spices, it was lean and good. But uneven cutting in the kitchen produced one piece of meat thicker than the others, and this was the only one that arrived medium-rare as I had requested. The others were those skinny pieces again. But my plate was full of other good things too. The pink rice had been cooked in tomato juice and the refried beans were rich and filling. With some guacamole and a small chicken enchilada in mole sauce, I was stuffed for $10.95.

For dessert, they make a dense Aztec chocolate cake (remember, chocolate was an Aztec delicacy) and a mild, milky rice pudding with lots of raisins. There's also vanilla custard, apple pie, and crêpes with a sweet goats' milk spread.

The Salt & Pepper must be doing okay. They opened a second location a while ago at 1609 - Centre Street N. (276-1010) and a third one at 2200 - 4th Street S.W. (245-6642).

MIDDLE EASTERN

BEIRUT

112 - 8 Avenue S.W. 264-8859

Lebanese. Mon-Sat, 11am - 9pm. Reservations accepted.
Fully licensed. Non-smoking section. V, M, AE. Take-out.
Summer outdoor dining. Cheap.

Stuck in the middle of Stephen Avenue Mall between a bank and a stereo store, the Beirut Restaurant is easy to ignore. We're used to brash fast food and happy hour places on the mall, not nice little cafés. Besides, the Beirut itself doesn't look like much. It's actually sort of homely and plain with its long white rectangular room, lack of decorations, and tables neatly lined up in three rows. But someone had the good sense to hang a huge red and white awning out front to open the eyes of passers-by.

It's impossible to eat at the Beirut without constantly comparing it to The Cedars, Calgary's first Lebanese restaurant. Many of the dishes are the same – falafel, the pungent mix of chick peas and spices; shawarma, marinated beef roasted on a vertical spit; and tabouli, a salad of crushed wheat, tomato, lemon juice, and parsley — to name just a few. And while you may not find the complexity and depth of flavour seen a few blocks away at The Cedars, the Beirut does provide a very fresh, clean tasting version of Lebanese food.

I like their hummus, a seasoned purée of chick peas and tahini (sesame seed paste). Not a difficult dish to make, theirs is one of the better ones around town. It's a light, creamy rendition that goes well dipped with wedges of pita bread. They make two other tasty dips — baba ghannuj, which tastes very much like the hummus only with a smoky eggplant flavour, and labne, a yogurt spread with mint.

There are usually some daily offerings like the lentil soup I had one January day. It really helped dispel the cold. Lentils aren't the tastiest things in the world, yet cooked in a broth with a whole mess of spices, they made a wonderful soup.

The most popular thing at the Beirut seems to be the chicken. The kitchen always does a superb job here. Big chunks of boneless chicken breast are marinated in a mixture of cinnamon, allspice, and a few other things and then charbroiled. It's really the tahini sauce that makes it though, spiked with the tartness of lemon and the bite of garlic. The finished product is available on a bed of rice or stuffed into a pita. Actually, most of the main courses come as a pita sandwich or with rice.

There are a few sweet desserts like baklava and crêpes covered in honey and pistachios, but there's nothing sweet about the service, or rather, the frequent lack of it. One or two of the staff know their business, but if you're not lucky enough to get them, you may find the service somewhere between oblivious and astonishingly surly. Staff sometimes congregate around the bar at the far end of the room, unaware of arriving customers. Be that as it may, if you're willing to persevere, you will be rewarded with very good food at quite cheap prices.

CAFÉ CERES

5, 201 - 10 Street N.W. 283-0964

Mediterranean with Turkish accent. Mon-Fri, 11:30am - 2pm, 5:30pm - 10pm; Sat, 5:30pm - 10:30pm. Reservations preferred. Fully licensed. No non-smoking section. V, M, AE. Moderate.

Café Ceres is probably the most understated and unknown place in the glitzy yuppie haven of Louise Crossing. Tucked into a corner of the strip mall at 10th Street and Kensington Road N.W., it hides away from the crowds. There are no neon or Christmas tree lights, just a small sign and a windowed storefront. Inside, it's a calm room with walls painted white and tables cloaked by lovely Turkish tapestries. It exudes a subtle eastern Mediterranean charm that provides a backdrop for a very lively, bubbly café. There's lots of laughing and boisterous talk here, and it seems to fit.

The menu continues that Mediterranean theme with a soft Turkish accent. There are peppers and yogurt, eggplant and calamari, herbs and spices. But the owner flexes her culinary muscles to develop new dishes. She creates delicate dishes with undertones of France and Italy. It is an evolutionary cuisine unique to Café Ceres. There's a very real commitment to quality and fresh products. Unsalted butter is sliced off a pound to serve in chunks, and plates are decorated with mint leaves or basil sprigs.

I started my meal with a cream of celery soup, surely one of the least inspired sounding soups going. That's why I ordered it. If you can make celery interesting, you've probably got a good restaurant. And it was lovely — thick, creamy, flavourful. Even my wife's ordinary-looking green salad packed a fresh, perfectly dressed taste.

We followed these dishes with one of the daily specials, chicken in a sour cherry sauce, and veal tenderloin roasted with dates, bacon, and pecans. If you like poultry in fruit sauces, this chicken is for you — not too sweet, not too sticky. The fruit enhanced the meat without disguising it. With a molded cup of rice prepared in chicken stock and sautéed carrots, it was a delicious meal. The veal, with savoury red pepper fettuccine, had been carefully combined with the other ingredients to create a delicately sweet yet smoky flavour. Unfortunately, this otherwise perfect dish had been overcooked for our tastes.

We finished off with pecan baklava and a lightly crusted crème brûlée that did not totally live up to its name. Although the custard was rich and smooth, there wasn't much of that notoriously brittle caramel crust that I enjoy shattering to then eat with the custard below. Regardless, we enjoyed an excellent meal that had, for the most part, been meticulously prepared.

With a selection of salads, pastas, and other entrées, from beef tenderloin with roasted peppers to lamb stuffed with hazelnuts and herbs, you can put together any type of dinner you'd like. You can lunch on entrées like croissants baked with camembert and tomatoes or Turkish böreks (phyllo pastry stuffed with daily savoury fillings) or chicken breast with spinach and gruyère cheese.

I have one small complaint: Although Ceres is comfortable, there does seem to be an airflow problem. It vacillated between very warm and almost chilly during our last visit, and the cigarette smoke from far corners managed to ignore the air cleaner and travel through the room quite easily.

Service at Café Ceres is professional and attentive. It got off to a slow start on that last visit, mostly due to a sudden crush of diners dropping in on their way to *Les Miserables*. But after they left, everything was fine. Don't expect your meal in a hurry though. Things take a while, but no longer than they should in a fine café.

THE CEDARS

1009A - 1 Street S.W. 264-2532

Lebanese. Mon-Thurs, 10am - 9pm; Fri, 10am - 11pm; Sat, 10am - 10pm. Reservations accepted. Beer, wine & liqueurs. Non-smoking section. V, M, AE. Take-out. Belly dancer for special occasions. Cheap.

Although other Lebanese restaurants have opened in Calgary, the best in my books is still The Cedars. A large part of its success is due to the friendliness of the Salloum family that runs it. Always cheerful and smiling, they instantly put their customers at ease.

This helps because when you join the lunchtime counter lineup, the overhead menu can be intimidating: shawarma, tabouli, falafel, tzatziki . . . It takes a while to read through. Long enough to raise the ire of any regular who's in the line behind you waiting to order his hummus and chicken pita. In this case, it's best to step aside, look helpless, and ask for explanations. If the staff have time, you may get an in-depth lesson in Lebanese cooking. If they don't, you'll at least end up with a plateful of fine tasting food.

The Cedars is a compressed restaurant without much room to move around, even though they have doubled their original size. It's always bustling, especially at lunch. They offer full table service after 5 p.m. with an expanded menu — a real menu that you can sit and peruse. Barbecued eggplant and zucchini, along with chicken, lamb, and beef kabobs, are added to the daytime list.

I always enjoy The Cedars' shawarma. Big chunks of mildly spicy beef are skewered and rotated on a vertical spit. As the meat roasts, orders are taken, and the cooked part on the outside is shaved off. Rolled into a pita with a tangy yogurt dressing and chopped tomatoes, lettuce, and parsley, you have a Middle Eastern dining delight. You also have one messy shirtsleeve if you don't hold it right. They're drippy little packages. If you don't want to risk a dribble or two, order the shawarma plate. It's served *with* a pita, not *in* a pita.

All of The Cedars' sauces are wonderful and carry an authentic level of spicing. If a dish calls for garlic and fennel, you get garlic and fennel. There's one thing to remember: If you're having a major afternoon meeting and you want to eat lunch here, invite your colleagues along. Either that, or stock up on breath mints.

Available all day and night are The Cedars' desserts — the honey-drenched baklava, the pistachio-filled knafi balls, the phyllo-covered ice cream, and many more. Perfect with a cup of dark coffee.

Prices have risen a bit over the past few years, but The Cedars remains one of the best places in downtown for lunch under $6. There's another location (called The Cedars Falafel Hut) in the MacEwan Hall food fair at the University of Calgary.

OLIVE GROVE

240 - Midpark Way S.E. (Midnapore Mall) 256-4610

*Lebanese. Sun, 4:30pm - 10pm; Mon-Wed, 11:30am -
12:30am; Thurs, 11:30am - 1am; Fri & Sat, 11:30am -
2am. Reservations preferred. Fully licensed. Non-smoking
section. V, M, AE, ER, DC. Take-out. Lounge with live
music Mon-Sat evenings & dance floor. Belly dancer Fri &
Sat evenings. Moderate.*

An olive grove in Midnapore? Yup, it's there all right. And it's healthy
too, having been around for ten years now. The Olive Grove serves
Continental food and stuff like steak sandwiches, chicken fingers, and
pizzas. But they haven't allowed these items to take over the menu. First
and foremost they are a Middle Eastern restaurant, with fare like the
eggplant pâté called baba ghannuj, the parsley and cracked wheat salad
called tabouli, the grape leaves stuffed with rice and beef called warak
arish, and the chicken breast topped with tomato sauce and cheese
called farouge m'sahab. And at least half their customers go for this
Lebanese cuisine.

That's what we did too. I opted to start dinner with a cold appetizer of
falafel, described as "The Middle Eastern Taco." That's probably the best
euphemism I've heard for this dish. Those who know it, love it. Those
who don't would be hard pressed to order deep-fried balls of chick peas
and fava beans. The Olive Grove serves theirs on a pita that is covered
with a chopped green salad in a creamy dressing. An excellent dish for
only $3.95. It could make a nice lunch. We also tried the kibbeh, ground
beef and cracked wheat with pine nuts, onions, and cinnamon. Not quite
as successful as the falafel as it was not uniformly hot.

Onc of the keys to Middle Eastern cuisine is the deliberate blending of
strong flavours. An able chef can work with them, producing pungently
mouth-watering dishes without a single aspect dominating. Fortunately,
the folks at the Olive Grove know how to do this, but they also know
what Calgarians want. I had the farouge mishwi as my main course.
That's half a chicken roasted with garlic and lemon and served with
vegetables and garlic paste on the side — a half cup of puréed garlic
seasoned with lemon and potato, among other things. Enough to ward
off vampires into the next century. I used maybe a half-teaspoon. If
you're a big garlic fan, this is great. If not, the chicken is well balanced as
it is. We also had the maklubi, thin slices of tender beef marinated with
cinnamon, sautéed, and served on a bed of rice and eggplant. It was
accompanied by a bowl of yogurt and topped with tons of pine nuts that
had been fried in butter, a perfect blend with the meat and eggplant. All
the trendy California places that sprinkle five or six pine nuts on plates
should take note.

I'm very impressed with the cooking here, not to mention the service,
which is efficient and discreet. Whether you're just having a pizza or

going for the Middle Eastern feast, they treat you well.

The main room is an interesting collage of pseudo-Mediterranean ruins, heavy tapestries, and private booths. Also of note is their non-smoking section, a separate room off the main dining area. Very elegant and quiet. It's softly overdone in dripping blue velvet with high-backed chairs and long-stemmed glasses. This isn't really necessary for the cuisine, but what the heck. It allows one to be comfortable no matter what the occasion.

I should mention the belly dancer on Friday and Saturday nights. With her ear-splitting finger cymbals and flashing bangles, she will interrupt your evening whether you want it interrupted or not. So, do what everyone else does. Smile uncomfortably and go with the flow.

ONE OF A KIND

AMADEUS

10, 7640 - Fairmount Drive S.E. 255-0563

*Austrian. Tues-Sat, open 5pm for dinner; Tues-Fri,
11:30am - 2pm. Reservations preferred. Fully licensed. No
non-smoking section. V, M, AE. Moderate.*

Amadeus is yet another example of a terrific restaurant situated in an
unusual location. Far away from any restaurant strip, it occupies the
south corner of a little mall that's kept busy by a bowling alley and a
balloon shop. It's dark and as soft as a duvet, with the feeling that it
belongs to someone who cares. It has the atmosphere of an Austrian
country inn with hand-painted decorations and freshly cut flowers.

Focusing on Austrian cuisine, Amadeus is popular for their schnitzels
made with good pork tenderloin. They used to have a Schnitzel Night —
now they have three (Tuesday, Wednesday, and Thursday). On these
evenings, there's a choice of eight schnitzels, from the simple wiener
schnitzel to the schnitzel Amadeus with Black Forest ham, bananas, and
cheese to the schnitzel Florentine with creamed spinach. I've had paprika
schnitzel that was tender enough to cut with a fork. Layered in a rich
brown sauce, it was surrounded by noodles and fresh vegetables. The
mushroom schnitzel is also very good, as is the jäger schnitzel in its
creamy vegetable sauce with spätzle dumplings.

Of course you can order off the regular menu on Schnitzel Nights too.
For those not interested in schnitzel, there are lamb chops, chicken breast
Florentine, smoked pork roll with sauerkraut, and a rich Zigeunertopf —
a traditional Gypsy pot containing chicken breast, peppers, mushrooms,
and onions in a pungent paprika sauce. Only slightly lighter are the lentil
and cream of asparagus soups and the baked mushroom appetizer. Even
the starter of broccoli toast is filling with its ham and cheese. But there is
a tomato salad.

Where Amadeus really excels is in its desserts. They're exceptional.
The Mohr im Hemd is a wonderful warm chocolate cake topped with
chocolate sauce and whipped cream. The apple strudel is at least two
inches high with apples, and the milchrahmstrudel is a custard-bread

pudding mixture baked in pastry and served with warm vanilla sauce and whipped cream. Incredible.

Service is always charming at Amadeus. It's a wonderful little spot with great atmosphere and terrific food. And it's a fine place to listen to the music of Mozart.

THE BAYOU

1901 - 10 Avenue S.W. 245-8833

Cajun & Creole. Sun, 5pm - 10pm; Mon-Thurs, 11:30am - 11pm; Fri, 11:30am - midnight; Sat, 5pm - midnight. Reservations recommended, especially on weekends. Fully licensed. Non-smoking section. V, M, AE. Lounge. Moderate.

The Bayou was an extremely popular little place on 11th Street S.W. until late August, 1990. Then, just as this book was going to press and shortly after I last ate there, it set up shop in a new location on 10th Avenue. Due to the timing of the change, I was unable to visit the new location. But the owners and the chef haven't changed, and the menu is the same. The decor will be different, there will be a lounge and maybe more elbow room, but look for that old ambience.

The Bayou is known for its Cajun and Creole food served in gargantuan portions. But it's an interpretation of southern cuisines rather than an adherence to specific preparations — you may find differences in style from what you've tasted elsewhere. And it's about the only place that has survived the passing of Cajun and Creole as a mainstream food fad. The chow is always consistent — I won't say stunningly great, but always good.

I know some people who never make it past the appetizer page. Barbecued oysters, coconut shrimp, gumbo, peppered redfish. All fine dishes. On that last visit, our half order of peppered shrimp included ten large ones swimming in a bowl of bitingly spicy sauce. More like a light dinner than an appetizer. The clam chowder was good too. We ordered a basket of their johnny cakes (deep-fried buckwheat dough balls) to go along with our appetizers. These little suckers are suppose to be firm, but the ones we got could have been whacked 150 yards with a five-iron. Great taste, though only good for dunking in the soup. Eaten alone, they would have been serious jaw breakers. We followed our soup and shrimp with a couple of Jamaican-style dishes, the jerk chicken and the jerk pork ribs. Both were okay. They came with different tomatoey sauces and huge piles of rice and spicy beans. But while the ribs were tender and juicy, the chicken was overcooked and dry.

There are lots of other good things on the menu. Creole-style paella, jambalaya, redfish Creole. It's real roll-up-your-sleeves food. Don't dress fancy here. This is full contact fare, and no matter how delicate you are, your partner will likely decorate you with part of his dinner. This too is part of the charm of The Bayou. I hope it remains at the new place.

Also at The Bayou are mega-desserts. Cheesecakes and man-eating pecan and apple pies were set out on the counter at the old place to tempt you.

Everyone leaves The Bayou with a doggie bag or two. If you can eat an appetizer, a main course, and some dessert, you should be trying out for the front line of the Stamps.

BOHEMIA BISTRO

Upstairs, 124 - 10 Street N.W. 270-3116

*Czechoslovakian. Tues-Thurs, 11:30am - midnight; Fri &
Sat, 11:30am - 1am. Reservations recommended. Fully
licensed. Non-smoking section. V, M, AE, DC. Summer
outdoor dining. Moderate.*

Bohemia Bistro. The name conjures up visions of beret-topped artistes swilling Absinthe while couples tango from one end of the room to the other. From the outside, the Bohemia Bistro fits the image with its narrow stairwell off the side of the building that leads up to the entrance.

But that's where the stereotype ends. Inside it's a squeaky clean, upscale place that could be renamed Café California. It's done in soft white and green with a beautiful black and white checkerboard floor. You almost expect The Great Gatsby to walk through the door. The tables are somewhat exposed, so it's not a terribly private place. But with enough customers and some jazz in the air, there's sufficient white noise to allow for private conversations.

The Bohemia Bistro features Czechoslovakian food, which shows strong Germanic and Slavic influences. With similarities to Hungarian, Polish, and Austrian fare, the emphasis is on hearty meats and stews. One item that distinguishes the food as Czech is the bread dumplings, made by rolling dough into log-shaped loaves, boiling them, and then slicing them. They're great. Probably three-million calories each once they've soaked up the creamy sauces. Another great Czech dish is the lentils served with bockwurst and sweet onion.

The pâté dumpling soup is especially good for soothing foodies who are tired of trying all the latest trends. It's "comfort soup." Four dense balls of beef pâté float about in a terrific beef broth. Very healthy. The chicken "whipprika" is not as spicy as a Hungarian paprikache, but is delicious with its creamy paprika sauce. Try it with those deadly dumplings. The "Spanish birds" are a Czech version of the German rouladen. Beef is rolled around bacon, onions, and pickles, smothered with herbs and Dijon mustard, and served with more dumplings and a creamy cucumber salad.

We don't have many Eastern European eateries around so it's easy to imagine a plate of boiled potatoes with slabs of meat thrown on top. This is hardly the case, and although the food at the Bohemia Bistro is far from delicate and low cal, it's very elegant. The Czech-born chef sometimes creates original California-style dishes too, bringing a lighter touch to the menu. And be it schnitzel or lentils or Caesar salad, the presentation is always pretty.

One of the bistro's best aspects is its outdoor café. Up there on the second floor, it's removed from the bus-stop syndrome of many others. It's a terrific place to pass a few casual hours surrounded by flowers and umbrellas and the trees of Louise Crossing.

CAFÉ DANOIS

500 - 5 Avenue S.W. (Chevron Plaza) 263-1114

Danish. Mon-Fri, 7am - 8pm; Sat, 10am - 3pm. Reservations accepted for dinner only. Beer, wine & liqueurs. No non-smoking section. V, M, AE. Take-out. Sat à la carte brunch. Cheap-moderate.

Looking for a good lunch place downtown? Tired of squishy sandwiches, watery salads, and all-you-can-eat buffets where you can't eat anything? Ever tried Café Danois?

It's been on the mezzanine level of Chevron Plaza for nine years. It's nothing ostentatious — in fact, it's easy to miss. A dozen or so tables are squeezed into a tiny room, with a few more outside the entrance. It's part cafeteria, part ship's galley — everything is compressed into the most efficient space possible.

During breakfast and lunch, patrons place their orders at the small opening of a counter stacked high with baked goods, coffee cups, and tea bags. They then move towards the cash register, gathering cutlery and condiments on the way. It looks disorganized, but it's actually extremely well thought-out. At lunchtime, for instance, you'll see a bunch of glasses on the counter already filled with ice, just waiting for the lunch crunch. The staff move slickly about, and the chef redefines the term short-order cook, pumping out a breakfast almost as fast as I can put cream into a cup of coffee and grab a morning paper off the wall rack. Café Danois operates in this cafeteria-style until 5 p.m. when table service commences.

The menu is designed for ease and flexibility but also to provide variety to the public. If your wish is not on the menu, just ask — they may be able to accommodate you or at least create something similar in moments. Danish cuisine is the specialty with things like red cabbage, Danish meatballs, and Danish open-faced sandwiches — these include smoked salmon with scrambled egg and onion, pickled herring with curry and apples, and roast beef with rémoulade sauce. More serious plates of steak Danois or deep-fried sole or homemade sausages are also available.

But they don't stop with the Danish fare. There's Caesar salads, Reuben sandwiches, and specials of teriyaki steak and lasagna rounding out the international side of the menu. Desserts are all done in-house too — muffins, cheesecakes, poppy seed cakes, apple cakes, and huge cookies.

The food is very good, fresh, and expertly prepared. Don't expect any frills, but do expect a heaping plate for a good price. It's simple fare prepared with flare, and if you can spend more than $25 here for two you're a much bigger glutton than I.

THE DEANE HOUSE

806 - 9 Avenue S.E. (Fort Calgary) 269-7747

Heritage Canadian & Afternoon Tea. Sun-Sat, 11:30am - 5pm. Reservations recommended. Beer, wine & liqueurs. Totally non-smoking. V, M, AE. Sept-early July: Fri murder mystery dinners. Cheap-moderate.

The Deane House Historic Site and Tea Room takes full advantage of Calgary's rivers. Situated at the confluence of the Bow and the Elbow, it commands a beautiful view of Fort Calgary and the downtown skyline. It's the former home of Captain Deane, Superintendent of the North-West Mounted Police. Built in 1906 and moved later to the east side of the Elbow, it's surrounded by huge trees and a garden. It's a grand old four-storey house with a large L-shaped verandah that has been glassed in and carpeted to hold the tea room. Antique tables and chairs, large windows, and old photos give it a relaxing elegance. As well as the tea room, the original dining room is open for special events such as weddings, and free tours of the house are available.

The level of professionalism in both service and food far exceeds what might be expected. The staff hustle about, occasionally missing a coffee refill, but dealing well overall. The newly renovated kitchen turns out Welsh rarebit, shepherd's pie, and a ploughman's lunch, bringing a turn-of-the-century British taste to the menu. It's a combination of traditional prairie squire dishes with more contemporary pastas, croissants, and quiches. A salad with warm breast of chicken and a pecan vinaigrette is delicate and lovely, and the vegetarian croissant is full of avocado, tomato, cucumber, sprouts, and cream cheese. During the summer, many ingredients come from the large and decorative garden out front.

The Deane House is at its best when it slows down for afternoon tea. It's the traditional style with fruit loaf, warm scones, little pastries, finger sandwiches and tea in dainty china cups. With butter and preserves, a full afternoon tea costs $6.95 a person (or an economical $3.50 for seniors). If you don't feel like you can eat all that, just try some fruit crisp or trifle or a basket of scones.

There are a few other things I like about The Deane House. One is the bathrooms. Outfitted with antique fixtures, they are a "must-see." (I understand that the ladies' even has a comfortable antique sofa.) Another is that the entire building, except for one tiny parlour, is non-smoking. It's good to see that they're preserving both our history and our lungs. And you can't beat a stroll along one of the rivers after tea. Whether you'd like to relive history or just watch the ducks, it's a lovely area.

FRANZL'S GASTHAUS

2417 - 4 Street S.W. 228-6882

German. Mon-Sat, 5pm - 1am; Mon-Fri, 11:30am - 2:30pm. Reservations preferred. Fully licensed. Non-smoking section. V, M, AE, ER, DC. Lounge. Summer outdoor dining. Live music & dancing nightly. Moderate.

Franzl's Gasthaus has been around for so long it's almost a forgotten ethnic restaurant. It's sat at the corner of 4th Street and 25th Avenue S.W. for twenty-five years, long before 4th Street became a trendy strip of restaurants. It serves good German food and *gemütlichkeit* — good times with friends. Upstairs you can warm yourself in the Heidelberg Lounge with a schnapps or two. The restaurant itself is downstairs in a large room with an almost community hall feel. It's flexible enough for weddings, birthdays, or Oktoberfest.

No matter how busy they get, it seems there's always room for more. We ended up there one night as the result of a rude maître d' at another restaurant. Not being fond of rude maître d's, we foraged out on a culinary challenge — showing up on a Friday night at 7:30 without a reservation. Franzl's was extremely accommodating, in spite of the fact that they were fully booked for Oktoberfest celebrations. They found us a quiet table in the corner and welcomed us as if we were regulars. And when our hostess saw that we had chairs she didn't like, she insisted on exchanging them for more comfortable ones.

Franzl's is a little piece of the old world with its schnitzel, sausage, and spätzle and its German-speaking staff dressed in Gasthaus tradition. Beer is available by the pitcher or the eighty-ounce glass boot as well as regular bottles and glasses, and there's a decent collection of German wines too. The wine is served from a *weinheber,* a tall glass contraption that works something like a coffee urn: You hold your glass beneath it and fill 'er up. And the food is good: hearty, heavy, and in line with an old Bavarian saying, "Meat is the best vegetable." But they haven't forgotten the vegetables. In fact, every spring they feature white asparagus fresh from Germany.

We started our meal with a collection of three salads: cucumber in a creamed dill sauce, a pile of pickled beets, and butter lettuce in a house dressing. All were excellent. We also tried the liver dumpling soup with a big pâté-like ball floating in a bowl of broth. Pretty rudimentary but very tasty.

We followed that with rouladen, a large slice of beef rolled around bacon, herbs, and a dill pickle and then smothered in gravy. Quite good, but it had fallen to the fate of many a rouladen — it was a little dry. We also had the schlachtplatte, or butcher's plate, an Oktoberfest special of bratwurst, weisswurst, other wursts, ham, sauerkraut, dumplings, and fried potatoes. It was great.

Franzl's is not a place for calorie counters. As we sat there, stuffed to the brim, they rolled the dessert cart by with its Black Forest cake, chocolate mousse cake, and other sweets. We couldn't possibly think of eating any, so we took some home.

The personality and service of Franzl's really makes it work. Everything runs like clockwork, but it's still so personable. I hope Franzl's is around for another twenty-five years.

LA PAELLA

800 - 6 Avenue S.W. 269-5911

Spanish. Mon-Sat, 5pm - 11pm; Mon-Fri, 11:30am - 2:30pm. Reservations recommended. Fully licensed. Non-smoking section. V, M, AE, ER, DC. Lounge. Moderate.

Spanish food has gotten an unfortunate short shrift around these parts — too bad, because I really like it. One real Spanish place is La Paella, a large restaurant with a lounge and a private function room. It has that distinctive mark-of-Zorro, hacienda look. Everything is red and white and black. Arched plaster walls and wrought-iron grills separate areas. Bullfight posters (the kind you get as a tourist in Spain with your name inserted for a small fee) line the walls. Sangria jugs and a figurine fountain add a touch that some call flavourful, others call tacky. Regardless, it's a comfortable room with its deep-red linens and oversized chairs, in spite of its obsessive air-conditioning system. (I like a well-ventilated room, but when napkins start to ripple in the breeze, I get a little concerned.) The waiters follow through with the Spanish image, wearing short red jackets, black pants, and a professional aloofness that contributes to excellent service that doesn't cloy.

They do their best business in the kitchen. We tried appetizers of prawns and scampi in different garlic sauces. That's one thing I like about Spanish cooking — lots of garlic. The half dozen prawns were excellent, fried in garlic and wine. The scampi were even better with a dose of Tio Pepe and butter. Both appetizers were served exceptionally hot in ceramic bowls — so hot, in fact, that when a chunk of bread fell in with the scampi by mistake, it became an instant crouton. Other appetizers include oysters, clams, and scallops. There are soups of gazpacho or lobster or garlic, and there's a traditional Spanish salad with salmon and boiled eggs.

For main courses, we tried some rabbit and the paella à la Valenciana. Rabbit dries out very easily, but this one, which we were told had been marinated for three days, was as tender as I've ever tasted. It came in a thickly herbed brown sauce with a bowl of roasted carrots, potatoes, and broccoli. The paella was the best I've had in years. Every chef seems to have his own version of this traditional Spanish rice dish, but so often in North America paella is devoid of moistness, with the rice turning crispy and the garnishes tough. For the most part, this one was fresh and moist. The chicken fell away from the bone, the clams and mussels were succulent. The only shortcoming was tough lobster. But the flavours were all there, with the customary saffron blending everything together.

Since we were celebrating a birthday, we indulged in not only a fine Spanish wine but some desserts as well. I had a slice of their lemon pie, which was mouth-puckering fresh. It had a nice texture, though the meringue was a bit too chewy. The other dessert was a bowl of crème caramel, ice cream, whipped cream, pineapple, and peaches in a rum sauce. Talk about decadent.

La Paella offers lots of other Spanish dishes too, like roast suckling pig (phone ahead for this one), cod in a tomato and red pepper sauce, duck in an orange sauce, or chicken in a mustard-garlic sauce. There's a few Continental touches like steak with maître d'hôtel butter or veal with crab and hollandaise. For lunch, there's even a Reuben sandwich. Still, the Spanish smells of olive oil and herbs ooze from the kitchen.

LE FLAMBOYANT

4018 - 16 Street S.W. 287-0060

French Creole from Mauritius. Tues-Thurs, 5:30pm - 9:30pm; Fri & Sat, 5:30pm - 11pm. Reservations recommended. Fully licensed. No non-smoking section. V. Take-out. Moderate.

When people ask me where to go for something really different, really good, and really exotic, the first place I suggest is Le Flamboyant, Calgary's only Mauritian restaurant. (At last count, there were only two or three Mauritian eateries in the whole country.) The reply is always the same. "Where is Mauritius? Where is Le Flamboyant? What is Mauritian food?"

Mauritius, at one time a French colony, is a tiny island in the Indian Ocean that is covered in sugar-cane and tea plantations. Due to its location and history, it has been influenced by not only the French, but by the Chinese, the Africans, and the East Indians. Consequently the food is spicy and rich with peppers, tomatoes, Creoles, and curries. Yet it can be smooth and delicate with béchamels and stocks. It's a wonderfully unique cuisine, perfectly executed at Le Flamboyant.

Le Flamboyant, named after the flame tree of Mauritius, is located in a little Altadore strip mall. Unassuming does not describe the understated atmosphere of this place. In the front room (the original room) there are four tables. A Mauritian beach mural covers one wall, and a seashell chandelier dangles overhead. It's a tiny space, so the family that runs the place built another room at the back a couple of years ago. This one seats about forty, and with lots of skylights, it's bright and cheerful. Le Flamboyant is not as opulent as some restaurants, but it's pleasant enough.

You won't find a more gracious host than Sybille Melotte, the elegant owner. This smiling, multilingual lady oversees everything herself. She shops for her ingredients, she cooks the food, she greets the customers, and she answers the phone. In many ways, dining at Le Flamboyant is like dining at someone's home. It's not impersonal or cold, but rather friendly and warm.

Her menu is short but incredible. The carrot soup is thick, creamy, and spicy. A green salad is drenched in a mouth-puckering mustard vinaigrette. There's a biting chicken curry, a piquant shrimp Creole, velvetty coquilles Saint-Jacques, and a bouillabaisse that defies description. This soup is loaded with seafood and layers of spicing that go on forever. On a recent visit, mine had chunks of crab and perhaps the best mussels ever. For dessert there are strawberry crêpes and brandy cake.

What I admire most about Madame Melotte's food is that it is uncompromising. She knows how it should be prepared, and she prepares it this way. It's balanced, it's clean, it's genuine. Some of it is too strong or too rich or too unusual for some people, but I love it.

Le Flamboyant is neither fast nor cheap. Almost everything is prepared to order, so it's not the place to eat if you are in a hurry. And because of the uncompromising quality, main courses run from $13 to $18. Not cheap, but incredible value. This is one of the best of the best restaurants in Calgary.

MIMO

4909 - 17 Avenue S.E. (Portugal Plaza) 235-3377

Portuguese. Sun-Thurs, 4:30pm - 10pm; Fri & Sat, 4:30pm - midnight (open for lunch by special arrangement). Reservations preferred. Fully licensed. Non-smoking section. V, M, AE. Lounge. Moderate.

Calgary is not exactly loaded with Portuguese restaurants. There is one. It's called Mimo, and it's difficult to find. If you can locate the Portugal Plaza at 48th Street and 17 Avenue S.E., you've got a head start. Then look for the Mimo sign and go through the door, past the bar, and down the hall to a pretty, windowless room. This is Mimo Restaurant where you'll find one of the warmest welcomes in town.

Renovations in the spring of 1990 brightened the room considerably. It's a clean white with green trim, crisp linens, and a mock skylight. A lobster tank guards the entrance, and two huge murals of the great outdoors sit behind fake windowpanes.

Mimo serves a delectable collection of Portuguese dishes. There are no non-Portuguese alternatives on the menu, so be forewarned. But even for the timid-of-taste, Mimo offers something.

One of the spicier dishes is the camarao ao alho, translated as garlic shrimp. The garlic is overpowered by the mouth-biting cayenne. These shrimp — fried heads and all — are coated red with pepper. They burn, they sizzle, they demand glasses of Vinho Verde to quench the fire. If the proper shrimp are used (sometimes their supplier doesn't come through), this is a compelling appetizer with the addictive blaze of good barbecued potato chips. Veterans suck on the heads to remove every last bit of spice. I've even taken the spent carcasses home to add to a Creole stock.

On the entrée side, the paella is very good if you're into a big seafood meal and a big price-tag at $29 for two. There's the pork and clam casserole (carne de porco a alentejana), a bizarre combination that works amazingly well. And there's various salt cod dishes that are far too salty for me. I think my two favourite entrées are the bitoque and the frango no chorrasco. The bitoque is simply prepared — a thin, fried steak served with french fries and a fried egg on top. Aside from the traditional ceramic platter, this looks like any steak and egg dish, but it has the taste of the Iberian peninsula. Whether it's the oil or the salt and pepper or the eggs, this dish tastes wholly different from what I'd expect from its appearance. The frango, my other fave, is barbecued chicken. Just about as deadly as the garlic shrimp, this is a half chicken coated in spices and roasted. If your mouth has been suitably numbed by the shrimp, you may not notice the burn, but if you're coming into it from a salad or a mild soup, watch out.

Dessert features an excellent crème caramel with a burnt-caramel sauce and the "house secret" Portuguese coffee — a few of these and you'll be dancing on the tables.

NATURBAHN TEA HOUSE

Trans-Canada Highway at Canada Olympic Park 247-5411

Eclectic (plus Light Lunch & Tea in summer). Sun buffet brunch, seatings at 10am, 11:30am, 1pm. July & August: Mon-Sat, 11am - 5pm. Reservations required. Beer & champagne. Totally non-smoking. V, M, AE. Summer outdoor dining. Moderate.

One of Calgary's best kept secrets has to be the Naturbahn Tea House. It's a tiny place perched on top of the ridge at Canada Olympic Park. When you enter the park, look up, way up to the top of the high-tech refrigerated bobsleigh and luge track. Just to the east sits a tiny chalet that accommodates the tea house and the start of the low-tech naturbahn luge track. Running down from the building in the summer, you can see a curving grassy trail, which when covered with snow and ice becomes the naturbahn (natural ice) course.

The tea house was first used for special functions during the Olympics. Now it's open seven days a week during the summer for Sunday buffet brunch, tea, and light lunches and the rest of the year for Sunday brunch only. It has, without a doubt, the best view of any restaurant in Calgary. Huge windows face west, north, and east down the Bow Valley. It's quite spectacular. The interior is decorated in cool blue and grey and pink with a slate fireplace. It's maintained the casual, outdoorsy attitude of the rest of the park, creating a family atmosphere.

The brunch is popular, so reserve ahead. Prices have risen since they began offering it — it's not as cheap as it once was. It's $11.50 for ages ten and up, $9.50 for ages five to nine, $10.50 for seniors, and free for ages four and under. Rather expensive for breakfast if you don't have a hearty appetite, but if you do, there's lots of good food.

It's a sizable spread of cheese, cold cuts, salads, fruits, hot items, and desserts. The salads are fairly typical — macaroni, coleslaw, that sort of thing — but nothing is floating in water or anything. They have conquered the problem of greasy sausage and rubbery eggs. I don't know how you can fill one of those steam trays with scrambled eggs and not have them vulcanize on you, but the Naturbahn has figured it out. Their bacon is crisp and their hash browns aren't too hashed up. The hot entrées are always good and include items like lasagna or rouladen. The dessert table is a real treat with various European pastries that actually taste as good as they look.

But brunch at the Naturbahn doesn't end with dessert. Although you can drive right up to the tea house, the best way to get down is with a casual stroll on the path beside the bobsleigh run. It's paved and quite negotiable for most people, though a few steep sections may prove difficult for some. If you're lucky (and it's between October and March), you might see some events or training runs — a great way to relive Olympic memories and impress out-of-towners.

ROCKIN' HORSE SALOON

7400 - Macleod Trail S.E. 255-4646

Western & Cajun. Mon-Sat, 4pm - 2am. Reservations accepted until 7:30pm. Fully licensed. No non-smoking section. V, M, AE. Licensed dance hall. Live music nightly starting at 8:30pm (cover charge Thurs-Sat after 8pm). Moderate.

I've tried to go to the Rockin' Horse Saloon around Stampede time without any luck. I couldn't even find a place to park the car. But things quiet down after the Stampede, and a person can actually get in.

The Rockin' Horse Saloon is a huge place, leading the trend in Western barn dance establishments. It's a restaurant, a lounge, a bar, and a dance hall all rolled into one and wrapped in oak, dark-green wallpaper, high ceilings, and country music. With Willie Nelson's nasal twang filling the air, guys in jeans kick their boots up on the brass rail. It's almost enough to take me back to my central Alberta CFCW roots — except none of the cheesy Western bars of my sordid youth possessed anywhere near the class of the Rockin' Horse. They had sawdust on the floor to soak up the Redman and Copenhagen juice and to hide whatever clung to your boots. The Rockin' Horse has carpet and attracts a cross section of country-music fans, from the yuppiest to the cowiest. It's brought country way uptown, and the food has moved with it.

The restaurant sits in a raised area on the east end of the saloon and overlooks the dance floor. It's almost an afterthought with only a dozen or so tables, but they do pay attention to it. This is not just a bar with a few tables in the corner serving greasy food. The tables are set nicely with linen tablecloths and napkins, and service is first-rate.

They've developed a menu that relies heavily on mesquite barbecuing and Southern U.S. cooking. There's lots of meat, hot spices and barbecue sauce, more meat, baked potatoes, and beer. Menus are printed on wooden breadboards, just like The Keg of yester-year. I suppose it adds to the down-hominess of the place.

Appetizers include cheese and mushroom soup in a bread bowl, seafood chowder, and deep-fried prairie oysters (not the real ones) wrapped in bacon. For the bar crowd, there are nachos and chicken wings from the universal chicken-wing vat — all chili and tabasco and fine with a jug of beer, but not great dining. There's a selection of salads with one of the worst Caesar salads I've tasted in years. It just plain smells and tastes bad. (I was told when I sent it back that it was made from a package.) Their garden salad, on the other hand, is excellent — lots of greens and vegetables all fresh and crisp. Simplicity itself, but something that boggles too many kitchens.

I was tempted by the buffalo steak, but opted for a dish called "Give Me Some Skin!" With a name like that it was tough to order, but I was won over by the thought of a boneless half chicken blackened in Cajun spices. The hard part about blackening food Cajun-style is that you have to throw the ingredients into a pan that's hot enough to smoke yet not inundate the kitchen. A lot of eateries back off on the concept, but not the Rockin' Horse. The chicken was thickly coated with spices (a bit too salty for me, but still nice) and juicy on the inside. Served with rice, carrots, and broccoli for $8.95, it was a darned good meal.

Other main courses include barbecued pork ribs or chicken, fried mushrooms on prime beef, and additional Louisiana dishes like blackened catfish and shrimp Creole. And there's deep-fried ice cream for dessert. Not much for wine, they serve predominantly domestic beer drunk from the bottle.

Aside from the food, the Rockin' Horse offers pool tournaments, dance lessons, and live entertainment. It's a fun, lively, loud place.

SULTAN'S TENT

909 - 17 Avenue S.W. 244-2333

Moroccan. Mon-Sat, 5:30pm - 11pm. Reservations recommended. Fully licensed. Non-smoking section. V, M, AE, DC. Take-out. Moderate.

A few years ago I reviewed a restaurant called The Casbah, Calgary's first Moroccan eatery. It's no longer around, but for once I wasn't too sad about the closing of a good place. That's because the people who ran it opened a new and better place, the Sultan's Tent. When the space on 17th Avenue that formerly housed Le Rendez-vous became available, they snapped it up.

Entering the Sultan's Tent is like crossing into the Twilight Zone. You step from the bustle of 17th Avenue, through a hand-carved doorway, and into the colourful sensuality of Northern Africa. It's dark, lit by odd-shaped lamps. Deep red and gold tapestries divide the room into small dining areas. A striped burlap cloth, alluding to the tent, is draped overhead, and it holds the soft Moroccan music inside. Moroccan artifacts, from a leather-covered desk to brass gunpowder holders, are everywhere. (There are no chairs here, and your table may just be a huge brass plate.) Every effort has been made to create an authentic look, feel, and taste, and the effect is stunning.

Four of us were led to a raised booth with padded benches and leather floor cushions. The two of us with bad backs lounged on the benches while the other two sank into the cushions. As we settled in, our waiter, definitely one of Calgary's best, brought menus and a wash basin. He then proceeded to pour orange-blossom water over our hands from an ornate silver urn. (Beats a hot towel any day.) That's because, in keeping with Moroccan tradition, the food is served for consumption by hand. Knives and forks are available, but if you're already sitting on a cushion, why not go the full nine yards?

The food fits the surroundings perfectly, with Moroccan delicacies such as the stew-like tajines, couscous specialties, harira soup made of lentils and chick peas. For the large-of-appetite, The Sultan's Feast is worth ordering. It's a six-course meal for a reasonable $22.75.

We started with the briq of mergues, lamb sausages wrapped in phyllo pastry. These were delicate and mildly spicy, served with a hot sauce called harissa for dipping. Excellent. Following that we shared the b'stilla royale, an interesting dish of cornish game hen, egg, onion, lemon, saffron, and almonds layered in phyllo pastry and topped with icing sugar and cinnamon. It's meaty, sweet, crunchy, soft — a terrific combination that can be an appetizer, a dinner in itself, or if pushed, a dessert.

After that we ordered their succulent lamb tajine, a fruity stew with prunes, apricots, and almonds. A similar rabbit tajine was not quite as good because the meat was dry. We also tried a savoury couscous with chicken and vegetables. The grain was perfectly cooked, and the meat awfully tender.

For dessert, there is an excellent baklava made with pistachios or a fruit salad. And then there is the super-sweet mint tea.

It's difficult to describe how fun and relaxing it is to dine at the Sultan's Tent. They spoil you with the food and the surroundings and the service. Our waiter, a Moroccan fellow who spoke at least four languages, was quietly entertaining enough to be worth the price of the meal alone. The only down note I can find about the Sultan's Tent is that it's so darned difficult to get off those benches after a two or three hour meal. Perhaps they could run a dinner-breakfast overnight special.

PIZZA

CILANTRO

338 - 17 Avenue S.W. 229-1177

Sun-Thurs, 11am - 11pm; Fri & Sat, 11am - midnight. V, M, AE, DC.

A wood-burning oven is the main feature of Cilantro's back room. Wrapped in white plaster with a tall chimney, it's surrounded by counters where the pizza chefs diligently work. The dough is flattened with a rolling pin so that the crust is thin, almost wafer-like if rolled too much. Decorated with pear, gorgonzola, black pepper, and pine nuts or pheasant, shiitake mushrooms, and asiago, this is not traditional pizza. But the toppings are so unusual that they work. (See full restaurant review in Contemporary chapter.)

CLAUDIO'S TRATTORIA

355 - 10 Avenue S.W. 234-0990

Mon-Fri, 11:30am - midnight; Sat & Sun, 5pm - midnight. V, M, AE.

Only a small part of Claudio's menu, these pizzas are memorable — lots of flavour is loaded on the chewy, bready crusts. They come in small, one-person rounds, but don't be afraid to share. Choices change monthly with seven types available at any given time. I like mine with basil, Roma tomatoes, and mozzarella or with Italian sausage and caramelized onion. If you can't decide, try the quattro stagione with four separate sections. (See full restaurant review in Italian chapter.)

ERCOLE

202 - 16 Avenue N.E. 230-4447

Sun-Sat, open 5pm for dinner; Mon-Fri, 11am - 2:30pm.
V, M, AE, DC.

For those into thick crusts, there's nothing chintzy about Mamma Erica's pizzas. They're almost over-topped with mega-cheese and other stuff. Among the best are the eight specialty pies, like the one with spicy meatballs or the one with fresh fruit and nuts. Pizzas are on the lunch menu, but you'll have to specifically ask for them at dinner.

Ercole has a new, impressively grandiose building with one of the best smoking/non-smoking divisions available — there's a room for each. And they have a lengthy list of hearty Italian food if you don't feel like pizza.

GALLO'S

815A - 49 Avenue S.W. (Britannia Shopping Plaza) 243-9307

Mon-Sat, 11am - 9pm. V,M.

Gallo's makes my favourite pizza. Their crust, the thin kind, is the best in town, and they use terrific toppings on it, like goat cheese and eggplant with sun-dried tomatoes or parmesan and prosciutto with basil. Sometimes they could lean a bit heavier on the toppings though. Oh, they also make the thicker-crusted versions, like the one with ham and pineapple. (See full restaurant review in Italian chapter.)

JENNY'S

8, 727 - 33 Street N.E. 248-0882

Sun, 4pm - 9pm; Mon-Sat, 11am - midnight. V, M.

A fluffy crust and tangy tomato sauce combine for a fine pizza. Nothing's overloaded here so each ingredient shows its own strength. Not fancy or outrageous. Just darned good pizza.

PIZZAMARIA

1010 - 1 Avenue N.E. 265-4440

Tues-Sun, 5pm - midnight; Tues-Fri, 11am - 2pm. V,M.

PizzaMaria used to have a lock on the title of Best Pizza in Calgary. The thin-crusted kind topped with capocollo and artichoke hearts and pesto and sautéed sweet peppers. Then the originators sold. But the new owners wisely persuaded them to pass on their secrets. So the pizza is still as good as before. Thick-crusted "regular" pizzas are available too, but try the thin ones. They're wonderful.

SPIROS PIZZA

1902 - 33 Street S.W. 242-5313

Sun, 4pm - midnight; Mon-Thurs, 4pm - 2am; Fri & Sat, 4pm - 3am. V, M, AE.

A change in ownership doesn't seem to have harmed Spiros at all. Perhaps it was time for some new blood. They still make one of the best, most heavily topped pizzas in town. Fans of the TV show *Twin Peaks* (Peakies as they are coming to be known) may want to try the one dubbed "Damn Good Pizza," though I'm not sure Agent Cooper eats pizza (unless he's a Teenage Mutant Ninja Turtle in his off hours, in which case he probably eats lots).

STARLITE

Heritage Drive & Fairmount Drive S.E.
(Acadia Shopping Centre) 255-3333

Sun & holidays, 4pm - 9pm; Mon-Sat, 11am - 1am. V, M, AE.

Many of the Starlite's smoked meat, artichoke, and onion pizzas have fuelled this book. Always with a good tomato sauce, a nice crust, and an excellent combination of mozzarella and cheddar cheeses, it's fine working pizza.

QUICK & EASY

AMANDINE

1600 - 90 Avenue S.W. (Glenmore Landing) 259-5864
2610 - Centre Street N. 276-3532

Call for hours. V.

Excellent cakes, fine tarts, nice nibbles, and baguette almost as good as Mont Blanc's. Probably the best donuts in town are made at the north location. It's a shame they don't show up at Glenmore Landing too.

BIG ROCK BREWERY

6403 - 35 Street S.E.
279-2917 (Office) & 292-7321 (Store)

Office: Mon-Fri, 8am - 4:30pm. Store: Mon-Sat, 10:30am - 6pm. No credit cards.

The best brew going. McNally's Extra Ale even made the cover of *The New World Guide To Beer*. They've branched out from their original line of ales to include XO Lager, dry beer, and designer labels — one of the most popular is Buzzard Breath Ale, served at Buzzards Café of course (and now shipped into the States). The ALCB-run beer store here carries a full line of Big Rock brews, and the office carries a line of beer goodies like glasses, t-shirts, and hats. Now your next party can look just like a beer commercial.

CAFFE BEANO

1613 - 9 Street S.W. 229-1232

Mon-Fri, 6am - midnight; Sat & Sun, 7am - midnight. No credit cards.

Schmoozing Uptown 17 and need a little eyeopener? Buzz into Caffe Beano for that caffeine pick-me-up — a double espresso for only a buck and a half. A few baked goodies and stuffed croissants will keep you from getting the shakes. There's café au lait, Vietnamese coffee, flavoured coffees, and decaf-uccino too. Grab some bulk beans to-go, all roasted by The Roasterie.

CALGARY'S FARMERS' OWN FARMERS' MARKET

5600 - 11 Street S.E. 243-0065

Mid May-mid June: open Sat. Mid June-late Oct: open Fri-Sun. Call for hours.

A new location has given this farmers' market more room, but has moved them off the beaten track. It hardly seems to hurt business though — the place really hops during the height of summer. Many local chefs shop here too.

Lots of seasonal produce is for sale. The best fruit and vegetables from Alberta and British Columbia are sold for good prices. Not everything is cheaper than you'll find at your grocery store, but if you're selective, you can find excellent quality. The product hot line above outlines the hours, how to find it, and what produce is available.

THE CHOCOLATE BAR

1431 - 17 Avenue S.W. 245-5013
9737 - Macleod Trail S.W. (Southland Crossing) 253-5586

Call for hours. V, M.

I though I lived a safe distance from The Chocolate Bar's 17th Avenue location. Then they moved a second one just down the street from me in Southland Crossing. Their market survey must have shown that I lived nearby.

Chocolate and cream in dozens of variations are the order of the day here, occasionally interspersed with nuts and fruit. They sell divine sweetness, plus more chocolate gift items for fellow chocoholics.

CHOCOLATERIE BERNARD CALLEBAUT

907 - 17 Avenue S.W. 244-1665
5403 - Crowchild Trail N.W. (Crowchild Square) 286-2008
1600 - 90 Avenue S.W. (Glenmore Landing) 259-3933

Call for hours. V, M, AE.

If you're going to eat chocolate, why not have the best? The packaging is gorgeous too. Callebaut's Belgian tradition of the finest, loveliest chocolates imaginable was carried to Calgary in 1983. Too bad they're so expensive, but once you've tasted them, you'll never go back to Black Magic.

DAIRY LANE MILK BAR

319 - 19 Street N.W. 283-2497

Mon-Fri, 7:30am - 8pm; Sat, 8am - 6pm. No credit cards.

This must be the last of the great tiny diners. The eggs and burgers are fried on a grill that looks centuries old. You can get decent milk shakes and soft ice cream cones. The stuff hanging on the walls and the folks behind the counter are worth the trip themselves. Their smiles are infectious, and their humour is right out of *Leave It To Beaver.* And the food is always good. Just like it tasted in the '50s.

DECADENT DESSERTS

924 - 17 Avenue S.W. 245-5535

Sun in summer, 2pm - midnight; Sun in winter, noon - midnight; Mon-Thurs, 10am - midnight; Fri & Sat, 10am - 12:30am. V, M.

Capitalizing on the public's weakness for sweets, this café is still pumping out Fantasy Fudge Cakes and 14-Karat Cakes like crazy. Cookies, pies, cheesecakes, and now milk shakes round out their repertoire. They come up with new concoctions to fit seasonal produce, like chocolate pâté with fresh raspberries. You'll see their desserts in other eateries around town, but it's always good to go directly to the source.

DIVA COFFEE ROOM

1154 - Kensington Crescent N.W. 270-9422

Sun, 10am - midnight; Mon-Fri, 7am - midnight; Sat, 9am - midnight. No credit cards.

Seen the big new green and red wedge building in Kensington? It's Calgary's answer to The Flat Iron building. Squeezed into the main floor "prow" is Diva, a place for coffee, cakes, and a read. The bowls of café au lait are pretty good, Sunday's *New York Times* well thumbed, and the view of Kensington entrancing. But some of the sweets taste like they're from an Easy-Bake Oven — all sugar and no flavour. Still, it's a good place for a caffeine buzz if you can't find room at The Roasterie.

DUCK WORTH FARM

17 Avenue S.E. (1 Mile E. of City Limit) 272-4100

Tues-Sat, 9am - 5:30pm. No credit cards.

How much is a duck worth? Certainly at least the drive out 17th Avenue S.E. Especially if you're tired of ducks with the texture of pink erasers.

Duck Worth raises and processes their own fowl, providing a quality frozen product at a good price. You can buy duck eggs and Alberta-made beef jerky here too, as well as all sorts of duck paraphernalia. And take the kids on a walk through the farmyard — there are lots of cute animals around.

DUTCH PASTRY
& CHOCOLATERIE

Britannia Shopping Plaza 243-4554
Crowfoot Plaza 239-3355
Market Mall 288-3814
Southcentre 278-5517

Call for hours. V, M.

It's always nice to find a bakery where the products taste as good as they look. Crusty dinner rolls, nougat cookies, oat bran muffins, cinnamon danishes — they all look and taste great here. Prices are up there, but I'd rather pay extra for quality than less for mediocrity.

4 ST. ROSE GENERAL STORE

2120 - 4 Street S.W. 228-1003

Sun, 11am - 6pm; Mon-Sat, 11am - 8pm. V, M, AE.

If you're looking for designer food, a good bet is the General Store, an amazingly practical place to power shop. Their in-house products are the best — marvelous jalapeno jelly, tasty corn relish, impressive baked goods. The mustards and vinegars can be had cheaper elsewhere, but they're still excellent for those last minute gift needs. And there are oodles of prepared foods to take home if there's a lineup at the Rose next door.

GERARD CHOCOLATIER

1, 338 - 10 Street N.W. 270-8438

Mon-Thurs & Sat, 10am - 6pm; Fri, 10am - 8pm. V, M, AE, JCB.

It was bad enough when Callebaut chocolates came to Calgary, but then Gerard's opened as well, offering more excellent chocolate and beautiful fillings. There's nothing artificial about these morsels either. You won't find a better raspberry filling anywhere. The pretty little shop and elegant owners make Gerard's a joy to visit.

GLAMORGAN BAKERY

37 Street & Richmond Road S.W.
(Glamorgan Shopping Centre) 242-2800

Mon-Thurs & Sat, 8am - 6pm; Fri, 8am - 9pm. No credit cards.

People still line up for their famous cheese buns, available with or without ham. No one else has been able to replicate them. Their Nanaimo bars and brownies are great too, as are their florentines. They're not always the friendliest people, but I suppose I'd get a little owly too if I had to work in such a hot place with so many customers. Make sure you take a number, and watch out for that step into the bakery. It's a real tripper.

GOURMET DELIS

Where does one find blue corn chips? Or herbed olive oils? Or smoked turkey sandwiches with mustard mayonnaise on corn bread or baguette? There are a number of excellent delis around town, but probably the four most popular are Peppers, Gourmet Royal, and Blue Vinny all in the Uptown 17 area and Lori's in Louise Crossing. The latest food trends are always on view and available for purchasing or just discussing. A visit to one of these places guarantees you'll be able to talk "food" with authority, and of course, it will brighten your dinner table.

Blue Vinny: 880 - 16 Avenue S.W. in Mount Royal Village, 228-5257, V, M. **Gourmet Royal:** 810A - 16 Avenue S.W., 228-1737, V, M. **Lori's:** 314 - 10 Street N.W., 270-4464, V, M. **Peppers:** 803 - 17 Avenue S.W., 229-2588, V, M.

HEARTLAND COUNTRY STORE

940 - 2 Avenue N.W. 270-4541

Café: Sun-Sat, 9am - 10pm. Store: Fri-Wed, 10am - 6pm; Thurs, 10am - 10pm. V, M, AE.

The concept is wonderful — a creaky, non-smoking, wood-floored building catering to the foot traffic of Sunnyside. There are muffins, coffees, magazines. Relax, browse through the crafts, select an herbed vinegar for tonight's salad.

HONG KONG BAKERY

110 - 3 Avenue S.W. 261-8853

Sun-Sat, 9am - 7pm. No credit cards.

Pork buns, ham and egg buns, beef curry buns — hot from the oven, slipped into a brown paper bag, they're great for snacking on down by the Bow. So are the cream buns — they have zero calories if you're walking on the bike path while nibbling. The Hong Kong was the first in what is now a booming Chinese bakery business in Chinatown. But it's still the leader of the pack for me.

LA RUELLE

Upstairs, 817 - 17 Avenue S.W. 244-6433

Mon-Wed & Fri-Sat, 10am - 5:30pm; Thurs, 10am - 9pm. V, M.

Looking for a café au lait or a citron pressé and a chat *en francais?* La Ruelle provides all the above (although it's predominantly a French bookstore) with a great view of the action on 17th Avenue. With a map of Paris in your hand, a little Piaf on the stereo, and baguette on the table, it could be any *petit bistro* in France. If only I could pay in francs.

MONT BLANC PASTRY SHOP

1403 - 8 Street S.W. 245-8448

Mon-Fri, 6:30am - 6pm; Sat, 6:30am - 5:30pm. No credit cards.

Mont Blanc bakes the best version of French baguette in town. The crust is usually crispy, the interior is invariably dense and spongy. It's perfect for spreading with sweet butter and Hero jam. The danishes and croissants aren't bad either.

MY FAVORITE
ICE CREAM SHOPPE

2048 - 42 Avenue S.W. 287-3838
755 - Lake Bonavista Drive S.E.
(Lake Bonavista Promenade) 225-1229

Sun-Sat, 10:30am - 10:30pm. V, M, AE, ER, DC.

Rork Hilford was the first person in Calgary to take ice cream seriously. (I'm not counting the notable efforts of MacKay's in Cochrane.) All the ice cream is still made to his specifications, and he still carries some exclusive flavours. Live piano, interesting goo-gahs, and Rork himself all add up to a fun time — and considering that the wait can be long, it's a good idea to have something to listen to or look at.

PIES PLUS

Macleod Trail & Lake Fraser Gate S.E.
(Avenida Bonavista Shopping Centre) 271-6616

Tues-Sun, 10am - 10pm. No credit cards.

Pie disappeared in the wake of trendy desserts, but it's making a comeback in the '90s. That's because few things can rival a fresh fruit pie, unless it's a fresh fruit pie with ice cream. Pies Plus is a spinoff of Just Pies Café in Bragg Creek, and it continues the tradition.

PORTUGAL BAKERY

3917A - 17 Avenue S.E. 235-0508
7013 - Ogden Road S.E. (called Ogden Bake Shop) 236-9616

Call for hours. No credit cards.

This is one of Calgary's best bread bakeries. And one of its cheapest. The buns, the Lisbon bread, the sourdough loaves are all lovely. Their excellent corn bread shows up in trendy delis around town. The cream-filled pastries are good too.

THE ROASTERIE

314 - 10 Street N.W. 270-3304

Sun, 9am - 6pm; Mon-Sat, 9am - midnight. V, M, AE.

The absolute best place in town for coffee beans. The smell of the roaster drags people along 10th Street into this tiny place. They churn out the beans (Montana Grizzly is my current favourite) and a great cup of coffee. On any marginally sunny day, dozens of people collect here and in the adjoining courtyard to sip bowls of café au lait (and smoke stinky cigarettes). Now if only they carried Mont Blanc's baguette.

SAUSAGE KING

Heritage Drive & Fairmount Drive S.E.
(Acadia Shopping Centre) 258-0228

Mon-Wed, 9:30am - 6pm; Thurs & Fri, 9:30am - 8pm;
Sat, 9:30am - 5pm. V.

Excellent German-style sausage here, tasting of herbs and quality meat. Gypsy ham, cured prosciutto-like pork, and wieners for the barbecue from these skilled sausage-makers show you what this stuff should taste like.

SIMPLE SIMON PIES

625 - Centre Street S. 237-0478

Mon-Fri, 9am - 5pm. No credit cards.

One of the oddest little joints in town, but their pies aren't bad. Made in single-serving sizes, a couple of these are adequate for lunch. There's curried lamb, ham quiche, raspberry, and many more. Usually a pot of soup is boiling over somewhere. Simon also shows up at Calgary's Farmers' Own Farmers' Market on Fridays and Saturdays (see entry in this chapter for hours and address). He also plans a new shop in Lake Bonavista Promenade in the near future.

WINE

The specialty wine business continues to be a vital addition to Alberta's culinary scene. **The Wine Shop** (815A - 17 Avenue S.W., 229-9463, V, M, AE, JCB) and **J. Webb Wine Merchant** in Glenmore Landing (1600 - 90 Avenue S.W., 253-9463, V, M) provide expert direction on wines.

Long the total domain of the ALCB, the world of wine is just starting to come out of the closet (or cellar, I suppose). The private shops bring in listings that the ALCB doesn't carry, allowing wine fans to concentrate on specific areas of interest. They also offer wine classes, tastings, and wine paraphernalia. They're always worth a quick browse to pass a few minutes.

SOUTHEAST ASIAN

BALI

5308 - 17 Avenue S.W. 242-5411

Indonesian. Tues-Sun, 5pm - midnight. Reservations recommended. Fully licensed. Non-smoking section. V, M, AE. Take-out. Pianist Fri & Sat evenings. Moderate.

The Bali has existed very calmly and quietly near the west end of 17th Avenue S.W. since well before the boom in Southeast Asian restaurants. The peanut sauces, satays, lemon grass, and sweet soy sauce have initiated many Calgarians to the food of Indonesia. Decorated with Indonesian shadow puppets, colourful masks, and a fearsome bird-like Hindu sculpture in one corner, the Bali has amassed a loyal clientele. The new subdivisions west of Sarcee Trail haven't hurt either.

It's a cuisine that relies on the intricate layering of fresh flavours. Sensations range from sweet to sour, spicy to suave. And vegetables play a prominent role. Gado-gado, for instance, is a mixture of various vegetables like potatoes, tomatoes, bean sprouts, green beans, and cabbage, all dressed in a piquant peanut sauce. The Bali excels at this dish. Sometimes their peanut dressing isn't as snappy as I'd like, but it's still a unique vegetable salad that peanut butter fans will enjoy.

The Bali's stir-fried prawns with pineapple swim in a tomatoey sauce that is smooth, sharp, and sweet all at once. Too much oil and too few prawns mar the dish, although the prawns that are present have been cooked to perfection. The sliced beef in curry is a decent, if fairly ordinary dish that doesn't live up to its billing as spicy. And the kitchen needs a heavier hand when it comes to adding lemon grass to the pork and citronella dish. The chicken, pork, and lamb satays with peanut sauce are always a good bet. The meat is marinated in ground coriander seeds and a sweet Indonesian soy sauce, so it's good even without the peanut dip. Every table has a container of crushed chilies, and I usually add some to my dip for a bigger kick.

The last time I visited the Bali, the service was so awry that it verged on humorous. Almost like a Keystone Cop flick. Too many overly concerned waiters were running about with too many pitchers of water, accomplishing little besides overflowing our water glasses a number of times. Our rice arrived after the other dishes, they brought us desserts that belonged to another table, it took forever to get our bill and even longer for them to pick up our credit card. While we waited, we watched three earnest waiters clanging and banging as they all cleared one table. And then when we ventured over to look at some of the Indonesian decorations on our way out, we were accosted by a distraught-looking waiter who wanted to know if he could help us. We left quickly.

Still, the Bali is one of a kind, and the fare is okay. Some dishes are better than others, as are some evenings.

THE CHILI CLUB

1312 - Centre Street N. 230-1100

Thai. Sun-Thurs, 5pm - 10:30pm; Fri & Sat, 5pm - 11:30pm; Mon-Fri, 11:30am - 2pm. Reservations accepted. Fully licensed. Non-smoking section. V, M, AE, DC. Take-out. Summer outdoor dining. Moderate.

The Thai craze has struck again — this time in the north. The address may look familiar to some because it used to house the original Chomps, one of Calgary's first restaurants to break out of the pancake house or Little-Joe-on-Bonanza mode. Chomps was a tight little place that served heavy-duty sandwiches, killer cheesecakes, and cappuccinos to the notes of Vivaldi and Mozart. Chomps was a big seller ten years ago, but trends come and go, and now it's Thai-time.

Mozart and Vivaldi still reign, and the small room is pretty much the same. Its finite interior seats forty-odd people, and the sidewalk café sprouts onto Centre Street. With so few seats, it's easy to keep a handle on the quality of food. And that has impressed me, and others, to date. A Thai friend rates The Chili Club as the most authentic in town. She tells me that the incredible strength of real Thai food can only be handled as a lifelong commitment and would be needlessly intense for infrequent imbibers.

We started our meal with some peek kai yod sai (I love the sound of Thai food). These deboned chicken wings had been stuffed with a mélange of chicken, shrimp, vermicelli, lime leaves, lemon grass, and spices before being deep-fried. Dipped in the best peanut sauce I've ever tasted, they were great. Four for $6.95 is at the top end price-wise, but they were primo quality.

We followed the wings with more fowl. In a creamy red curry sauce with peanuts, our panang duck had a mild kick, but was light on the duck. The eggplant in it was excellent, soaking up just enough sauce to complement itself. The pad kra pao kai, stir-fried chicken with fresh basil and chilies, had more of a bite and a cleaner taste than the duck. The

114

basil and chilies permeated the clear broth that coated the tender chicken. Sopping up all the flavours at our table were steamed rice and coconut rice. (We couldn't decide on which kind to order, so we tried both.)

The Chili Club has over fifty items. There are salads and soups, noodle and vegetarian dishes, and beef and pork and seafood concoctions. The staff are very adept at assisting and clarifying and even offering tastes of items. We wanted to know the difference between the tropi-tango and the mango ice creams, so our waitress brought us a spoonful of each. The tropi-tango combo of papaya and lemon won out, but the mango was good too.

There is one negative thing to say about The Chili Club: It has an unfortunate smoking/non-smoking situation. Although they do designate a very small section for clean air, it's such a tiny restaurant that it makes no real difference if someone does light up.

Regardless, The Chili Club is an impressive addition to the Thai dining scene. And it's nice to stay north of the river to indulge in this cuisine.

THE KING & I

822 - 11 Avenue S.W. 264-7241

Thai. Sun, 4:30pm - 9:30pm; Mon-Thurs, 4:30pm - 10:30pm; Fri & Sat, 4:30pm - 11:30pm; Mon-Fri, 11:30am - 2:30pm. Reservations recommended. Fully licensed. Non-smoking section. V, M, AE. Lounge. Take-out. Moderate.

When I first saw The King & I, I doubted its authenticity. The name immediately brought visions of Yul Brynner and Deborah Kerr in the movie of that name. The decor was generic high-tech, plus the staff seemed distinctly non-Thai. So I was anticipating a pretty dull, white bread version of Thai food.

Was I surprised. Focussing on freshness and providing a cross-section of Thai food, The King & I offered a balanced, often jumpingly spiced selection. Since that first impression, The King & I has moved next door to a larger location that still looks as though they could be serving Italian or Mexican or Middle Eastern without changing so much as a light bulb. But it's pleasant, the menu has grown, and the food itself is still excellent.

Thailand is wedged into the heart of Southeast Asia and lies close to both India and China. As such, its cuisine shows similarities to those of its neighbors. There are curries, there are satays, there are spicy ginger sauces. The King & I goes for a "best of " collection, which they say is as authentic as possible. Never having been to Thailand, I'll take their word for it. They serve their dishes in larger, North American-appetite sizes, and they apparently tone down some of the spicing for Canadian palates.

But the flames can still be substantial, so you might think twice before asking them to step on it.

We started one meal with some nung goong, shrimp and pork dumplings with a lime and chili sauce. This was the least impressive of our dishes. The meat mixture was just a lump of processed protein without a distinct flavour, and the dough was slimy. The lime-chili sauce refreshed our taste buds, but not enough to save the dish. Then we tried the ka ree moo, pork and honeydew melon in a yellow curry. Smoothed with coconut milk, it was an excellent combination, if a trifle light on the pork. From the vegetarian list we ordered the yam hed, a tangy bunch of fresh mushrooms and green onions in Eastern spices. Very nice. The highlight had to be our pad kai long song, a dish of boneless chicken and spinach in a hot peanut sauce. While the chicken was tender and hot, the spinach had barely been cooked, giving it just a little crunch and a lot of flavour. The peanut sauce added a layer of spice over the cool spinach and moist chicken.

Lunchtime features combo plates of two or three items, or you can belly on up to a Thai buffet for $7.95. The dinner menu contains over sixty dishes. Most fare is listed under its Thai name, with the exception of a few like "Thai sticks" or "rock and roll clams" (just to keep you awake I suppose). Dinner for two, without wine, will set you back around $40 or $50, so The King & I is pricier than its sister eatery next door, You're So Sweet Noodle House.

LITTLE BANGKOK

720 - 8 Avenue S.W. 264-8725

Thai. Sun, 5pm - 9pm; Mon-Fri, 11:30am - 11pm; Sat, 5pm - 11pm. Reservations recommended, especially for large parties. Fully licensed. Non-smoking section. V, M, AE. Lounge. Take-out. Moderate.

A few years ago in Calgary, you couldn't get a mee krob or por pia tod to save your life. But then the Little Bangkok Thai Experience opened up, showing us what the latest rage was all about.

The food at Little Bangkok emphasizes the working-class vein of Thai cooking, with big chunks of things, thick sauces, and robust flavours often hot enough to burn your lips off. They use tons of peanuts, coconut milk, curries, and chilies, and there are lots of interesting items on the menu. Like chicken sautéed with green curry paste, coconut milk, snow peas, and lemon leaves. Or beef with green peppers, basil, onion, and chilies. Thai cuisine is similar to those of other Southeast Asian countries, and lovers of East Indian and northern Chinese food will like it.

It's too bad Little Bangkok inherited the space that formerly housed the infamous Tiki-Tiki, a popular joint in the '70s when pseudo-

Polynesian food, plastic fronds, and little umbrella-adorned drinks were in vogue. The Tiki-Tiki's popularity dissipated in the wake of widening tastes, but the decor lives on like a zombie in a '50s horror movie. It's still too dark. Those thick wooden tables with holes gouged out for seashells are still there. And although new Thai murals adorn the walls, bamboo thatching still covers the ceiling. It's sort of like dining on the set of *Gilligan's Island*.

But the food more than compensates for the surroundings. We tried some por pia tod, Thai for deep-fried spring rolls. Although these weren't as exceptional as the rest of our dishes, the rolls were very palatable and made tastier by the addition of two sauces. We had a couple of lukk chin ping, which were little grilled meatballs. Though we were advised that most people didn't like their rubbery texture, we quite enjoyed them. Next we discovered the yum neau, an outstanding salad of grilled beef slices, cucumbers, and lettuce doused with fresh herbs, crushed peanuts, and lime juice. Great value for only $6.95. Dishes are marked with one, two, or three flames to designate hotness, so we tried the two-flame kai curry, chunks of chicken sautéed in coconut milk and yellow curry paste. It too was very nice, but the chicken suffered from a brutal chopping. The one-flame Thai ginger pork was served with a slew of ginger, onions, and mushrooms in a pungent and biting sauce. Another excellent dish. I'll pass on further desserts after trying a bowlful of tapioca, peanuts, and hot bananas. It didn't taste too bad, but it was one of the homeliest things I've ever eaten.

One other appealing aspect of our meal — aside from the fact that all those dishes covered the seashells in the table-top — was the rice container. An elegant aluminum bowl, it stood about fifteen inches high. And here's a note on eating Thai: Although the food is served for sharing, a spoon and fork, not chopsticks, are the utensils of choice.

So go try some goong nam prigpow or some hoy mang poo. But don't say I didn't warn you about the decor.

ORIGINAL PHNOM-PENH

1209A - 1 Street S.W. 233-0768

Cambodian, Vietnamese & Chinese. Mon-Fri, 10am - 10pm; Sat & Sun, 10am - 11pm. Reservations accepted. Fully licensed. Non-smoking section. V, M. Take-out. Cheap-moderate.

The family that runs the Original Phnom-Penh originally came from the Chiu Chow region of southeastern China, but they settled in Cambodia for a couple of generations. They ended up in Canada (and eventually Calgary) after a short stop in Vietnam. They're serving another variation of Southeast Asian cuisine to Calgarians, one that mixes their

Chinese descent with their Cambodian and Vietnamese heritage. I tried one of the Cambodian noodle soups. It was a light, clear broth filled with noodles and roast pork. With a couple of large shrimp and a huge meatball similar to the filling in Peking dumplings, it was a meal in itself. Spiked with fresh green onions and cilantro, it cost only $4. An amazing deal.

There are fifteen other soups on the menu, ranging from juicy beef ball soup and perfume duck soup to wonton and a Cambodian-style hot-and-sour. There's an interesting selection of other dishes that I haven't seen elsewhere in town. Like golden crispy oyster cakes or baked prawns with rock salt or vinegared asparagus.

I also ordered a familiar item, the Vietnamese cha gio (spring rolls filled with minced meats and vegetables, wrapped in mint and lettuce, and dipped into a spicy fish sauce). Lots of fresh mint cut through the residual oil, and the filling was excellent. Like most places that offer these things though, there wasn't enough lettuce. But they were served incredibly hot — it looks like things come directly from the stove to your table, which is nice to see. Everything except perhaps the deep-fried ice cream I had for dessert. A big ball of ice cream had been coated with a corn dog-type batter and deep-fried. I think it had been done earlier though, because the exterior wasn't warm at all. It had the slippery, fried texture of a day-old chicken ball. The ice cream was good, basic vanilla, but forget the coating.

The Original Phnom-Penh's location, on the ever-changing 1st Street strip, has seen more restaurants than I care to count. I hope the Phnom-Penh can stick around. If first impressions and an almost overly efficient staff are any indication, they have a good chance.

SAIGON

7, 575 - 28 Street S.E. 235-5757

Vietnamese. Sun, 10am - 10pm; Mon-Sat, 11am - 11pm. Reservations preferred for groups. Beer & wine. Non-smoking section. V, M, AE. Cheap-moderate.

One of the best restaurant tips I've ever received was that a new Vietnamese place had opened in the Southeast. The Saigon is located off Memorial Drive on 28th Street S.E. in the heart of Calgary's Vietnamese community. This ensures a good level of authenticity and, hopefully, a steady clientele. If you're not from these parts, it's only seconds off Deerfoot Trail and worth the trip if you're looking for a distinctive meal.

Vietnamese food is refreshing when properly prepared, and the Saigon's cha gio (Vietnamese spring rolls) typifies this aspect of the cuisine. A mixture of ground pork or chicken, vegetables, spices, egg, and vermicelli is rolled inside delicate sheets of rice paper and then deep-fried. To eat, you wrap these sausage-like creations in mint and lettuce and dip in a tart vinaigrette made with nuoc mam, the ever-present Vietnamese fish sauce. They are light and tasty, and each ingredient manages to maintain its own flavour. An order of five costs an amazing $3.25. There's about a buck's worth of mint alone.

The sweet-and-sour shrimp comes with a dozen or so large shrimp sautéed with vegetables in a light, tangy sauce. It's very tasty. The fried noodles with vegetables is a nice, but fairly ordinary dish. To try the spicier side of this cuisine, sample the citronella chicken. Presented inside a ring of cucumber slices and sprinkled with peanuts, it is a pretty dish that bites a bit. One of my favourites is the bo tai chanh, quick-fried, lean beef with lime and onion. Lovely and fresh. If you're into do-it-yourself meals, try one of the Genghis Khan grills. You cook marinated beef, shrimp, or squid over a hat-like contraption at the table and then wrap it inside rice paper along with mint, vermicelli, and bean sprouts. Lots of fun.

French involvement in Vietnam left its mark on the cuisine. You can see it in the Saigon's menu with items like pork "brochettes," frog legs fried in butter, and bananas flambéed with French brandy.

You might find the servings at the Saigon a little small, but the quality is definitely there. And presentation-wise, this food rivals Japanese. The dishes are laid out with care and expertise. The only fault I can find is that sometimes the dishes are served in the wrong order, with the spicier ones coming ahead of the relatively tame ones.

The Saigon is a fairly casual place. There's a wall of mirrors, a few plastic plants, and some Vietnamese pictures. If it's a little stark, the friendliness of the staff adds some warmth. And if they don't warm you up, try those flambéed bananas for dessert. They are a nice change from the brace-locking toffee bananas of Peking cuisine.

SIAM SUKIYAKI

351 - 10 Avenue S.W. 266-5808

Thai. Mon-Thurs, 5pm - 10pm; Fri & Sat, 5pm - midnight; Mon-Fri, 11am - 2pm. Reservations recommended on Fri. Fully licensed. Non-smoking section. V, M, AE. Moderate.

Siam Sukiyaki. It sounds like an ultra-cute name for a Thai restaurant, perhaps chosen for its cadence and rhythm rather than its significance. We've come to know sukiyaki as a Japanese dish, not a Thai one. I am told, however, that sukiyaki refers to a form of fondue native to Thailand and the house specialty at Siam Sukiyaki.

Siam Sukiyaki is located on 10th Avenue S.W. between 2nd and 4th Streets, and as such, it's physically about halfway between two other Thai restaurants — The King & I on 11th Avenue and Little Bangkok on 8th

Avenue. It's also about halfway in terms of decor. Not as upscale as The King & I or as earthy as Little Bangkok, it covers a comfortable middle ground. I'm glad these guys aren't just trying to copy each other. The decor at Siam Sukiyaki is in a bit of a beach-hut mode, with a bamboo roof hanging over a raised seating area in the middle. Left over from the previous resident, Pearl of Orient, this upper level neatly halves the restaurant into smoking and non-smoking sections and creates a place to put the buffet.

Every weekday Siam Sukiyaki offers a lunch buffet — all you can eat for $6.95. This is an excellent way for a restaurant to introduce customers to their food and their establishment, and a deal like this attracts customers even when they can't pronounce the names of the dishes. Whenever I've been at Siam Sukiyaki for lunch, it has been very busy, with almost everyone going for the buffet. I tend to avoid smorgs, but this one is tempting, with things like Thai spring rolls, sliced beef in yellow curry, crispy egg noodles with shrimp and pork, and blazing coconut chicken soup. It's fundamentally a good spread, but suffers the same problem as any buffet. After the food sits in those warmers for ten minutes, it starts to deteriorate. Ordering off the menu is fresher but not as cheap.

Thai food can be amazingly fiery, yet some dishes will have no flames at all. The fifty-two item menu at Siam Sukiyaki runs the whole gamut and divides the spicy food into three levels by the allocation of stars. A plate of four chicken wings is one of the non-spicy items. To my amazement, these have been deboned and then stuffed with pork, noodles, and lemon grass for an impressive $5.95. And then there are the deep-fried quails. A true treat.

The steamed shrimp salad is an outstanding one-star (meaning spicy) item. A half dozen shrimp are steamed and mixed with red onion, celery, carrots, and lettuce and drenched in a lime-mint coriander dressing. The shrimp pick up a tartness and practically explode your mouth with flavour. I've also tasted the three-star (fiery hot) chicken with onion and string beans and the two-star (very spicy) pork loin with green peppers, onion, chili, and basil. Although I didn't detect a noticeable difference in heat between the two, both dishes had strong, distinct flavours. And even though the sauces were very spicy, the individual nuances of the most delicate vegetables came through.

Siam Sukiyaki's prices are good — less expensive than The King & I and on par with Little Bangkok. A lunch of three dishes and a big aluminum pot of rice is just over $20. With the quality of food they put out and the friendly, accommodating staff, Siam Sukiyaki is sure to be around during the post-Thai food craze, whenever that may be.

THE SIZZLING WOK

1312 - 12 Avenue S.W. 228-1611

Malaysian. Sun-Sat, 4:30pm - 11pm; Sun-Fri, 11:30am - 2:30pm. Reservations preferred, especially Fri & Sat evenings. Fully licensed. No non-smoking section. V, M, AE. Lounge. Take-out. Summer outdoor dining. Sun buffet brunch. Moderate.

Time was when The Sizzling Wok was an exotic, unusual restaurant. It was one of the first Southeast Asian eateries in Calgary, presenting Malaysian food with names like daging rendang and minangkabul chicken. It offered an adventure in dining and a conspiratorial atmosphere among the patrons who congregated there. It also offered an adventure in parking, pushed up against Edmonton Trail in a building that could just as easily have warehoused auto parts. Back before Bridgeland started gaining its fashionable cachet, this was the wrong side of the river. The dark, grotty look of The Sizzling Wok was perfect for the times. We're not talking that long ago. About '82 or '83.

But times change and so has The Sizzling Wok. It's moved across town into a room on the ground level of an apartment tower. This space has had at least three previous incarnations, but I think The Sizzling Wok is there to stay. Partly because the proprietors have gone beyond their Malaysian theme (which isn't all that unique anymore) with the Satay Lounge, a typical big-screen-TV-with-happy-hour kind of place. And partly because the food is still pretty good.

Nicely separated from the lounge is the restaurant, a bi-level room decorated in soft greys and blues with tablecloths, comfortable chairs, and Malaysian batiks. This is a real change from the past. It's actually quite pleasant, with its wall of south-facing windows and sidewalk café.

We started our meal with an order of satay, bits of pork that had been skewered and grilled. A half dozen for five bucks. Not bad, but not as generous or juicy as I remember from the old days. And they seemed a little greasy. The peanut sauce seemed toned down too. I was starting to think that the old Wok had slid downhill in its new trappings until they brought out our main dishes of nasi goreng, asam udang goreng, and sizzling drunken chicken. These were all good.

The nasi goreng was a lightly fried rice dish with some vegetables and big chunks of chicken and beef, providing an appropriate contrast to the asam udang goreng, a collection of prawns steeped in a curry sauce. Not a hot, biting curry, just smooth and rich. The drunken chicken wasn't impaired at all on the scale of culinary acceptability. The chicken was extremely tender in its smooth, tangy, garlic-wine sauce, surrounded by pea pods, mushrooms, and water chestnuts. Excellent.

The similarity of Malaysian food to that of Chinese, East Indian, and Indonesian is apparent here with items like deep-fried wontons, hot-and-sour soup, more curries, and gado-gado (a typical Indonesian vegetable salad with a peanut dressing). There are oodles of soups and noodles, a plethora of chicken and shrimp, lots of vegetables and beef, and a nod to lamb.

Most of the changes at the new Sizzling Wok are welcome. But it's funny how some niceties, like tablecloths, can become problems. Sizzling hot plates are, by definition, a bit messy, and The Sizzling Wok serves a variety of them. The waiter places a screaming-hot cast iron plate on your table. Then a dish of food is dumped on it, causing a huge sizzle and lots of splatter. That's fine as long as you aren't wearing silk or can duck fast, but it does play havoc with the tablecloths.

TRONG-KHANH

1115 - Centre Street N. 230-2408

Vietnamese. Sun-Thurs, 10:30am - 9pm; Fri & Sat, 10:30am - 10pm. Reservations accepted. Beer & wine. No non-smoking section. V, M. Take-out. Cheap.

The Vietnamese restaurant business is steadily growing these days now that a lot more of the public are trying this food. That's great because it's such a fine cuisine.

The Trong-Khanh falls into the category of a Vietnamese noodle house or diner as opposed to more upscale places like the Saigon or A Touch of Ginger. It's a homely little place on Centre Street, decorated in basic red and white — red vinyl chairs, white bumpy brick walls. It's got a sparse, linear look with glass-topped tables lined up in rows and a big pop cooler sitting in the middle of the room. That cooler has seen better days as evidenced by the strange sound it emits — sort of like a UFO from a '50s Sci-Fi movie. Just as odd is a huge set of horns over the entrance to the kitchen, either from a longhorn bull or a water buffalo. In relation to the rest of the decor, which is almost nonexistent, these really stand out. But the sparseness of the surroundings does not detract from the food.

The Trong-Khanh has eighty-three items on the menu, and I have barely begun to sample them. It's a basic list of soups, with or without noodles, various other noodle and rice offerings, and a short list of what they call dinner dishes, like sparerib stew or fried shrimp and vegetables. In the area of appetizers, they include ground shrimp wrapped with sugar-cane, fried egg-cakes, and of course, the spring rolls called cha gio. Wrapped in rice paper, their cha gio are larger and more meaty than most. But served with lettuce and basil leaves for wrapping, they're still light and fresh. And at only $2.50 for four good-sized rolls, it's a really cheap and tasty way to start a meal.

I'm told that the soups are very good, especially the Cambodian noodle one, but I went for a big ticket item, the $6 lemon grass barbecued chicken. Large chunks of skinned, sliced, and deboned chicken are flavoured with lemon grass and lime and barbecued on skewers. Charred chicken and lime combine wonderfully here. To complement this dish, I ordered the fried noodles with shrimp and vegetables — a big pile of vermicelli with a half dozen large shrimp and lots of fresh broccoli, carrots, and onion in a slightly thickened chicken stock. A lot of food for $5.50.

The fare here is straight ahead and simple. It lacks the subtlety and complexity of more sophisticated Vietnamese places, but it maintains the freshness and quality. For a quick meal at a decent price, the Trong-Khanh has a lot going for it.

Also on the plus side are the people, a young bunch who are trying hard. They appear a little inexperienced at coping with complex orders and requests. Nonetheless, I think they deserve a chance.

YOU'RE SO SWEET NOODLE HOUSE

818 - 11 Avenue S.W. 269-5366

Southeast Asian. Sun, 4:30pm - 9:30pm; Mon-Thurs, 4:30pm - 10:30pm; Fri & Sat, 4:30pm - 11:30pm; Mon-Fri, 11:30am - 2:30pm. Reservations recommended. Fully licensed. Non-smoking section. V, M, AE. Take-out. Moderate.

A couple of years ago the hot new restaurant to hang out in was The King & I Thai Cuisine. It got so popular so fast that it moved into a larger space next door, freeing up the original room. Rather than desert the old spot entirely, the owners opened another restaurant in it.

This one goes by the unwieldy name of You're So Sweet Noodle House. Not exactly my first choice for a blind date, but then I'm already married, and I guess it does grab your attention. It looks just like it used to — a long, narrow room with a small front section on the ground level coupled with another section up a set of stairs. The ceilings are open way up to the beams. Large monochromatic banners dangle down, moving in the air to create an image of kites flying overhead and a feeling of openness that is welcomed in the cramped seating area below.

The menu is different from The King & I, focussing on a more general style of Southeast Asian cooking, but it still keys in on their success. The dishes here are simpler and cheaper and, guess what, lots of them have something to do with noodles.

Of those that don't, there are delicious beef or chicken satays, marinated and skewered meat served with a peanut sauce hot enough to curl your toenails. There's a bunch of mild Japanese curries that don't contain any dairy products and are apparently all the rage for lunch in Japan right now. The pot stickers, with their ginger-lime dip, are sort of Peking dumplings à la Southeast Asia.

The appetizers at You're So Sweet are hard to pass up. Aside from the satays and pot stickers, there are imperial rolls and salad rolls, both featuring noodles and chopped meats wrapped in thin rice pancakes. The main difference between the two is that the imperial rolls are deep-fried.

Past the appetizers, I've tried the oyster chicken salad. No oysters in this, just a tangy oyster sauce. And lots of chicken, sprouts, noodles, and a big pile of cashews. This is a warm salad with a crisp, sharp bite and loads of flavour.

I've had the Shanghai-style noodles, a spicy dish with lots of great chicken, shrimp, and squid — nothing rubbery here. And I've pigged out a few times on the peanut chicken fettuccine, served like many of the other dishes on a decorative bed of lettuce. It's maybe a little odd to see fettuccine on the menu, but it works really well.

Service at You're So Sweet follows the quality of the food — very friendly, very professional, a little on the trendy side, but very accommodating. They're proficient at delivering the dishes the way you want — one at a time or all together. On a recent visit with a group, we ordered six dishes and were served by a different staff member each time. But we got *what* we ordered *in* the order we ordered it, so who can complain?

Prices aren't bad either. Two can eat quite nicely for under thirty bucks, and there's an early bird special from 4:30 p.m. to 7 p.m. that features entrées at only $5.95.

BANFF & BOW

CORRIDOR

BALKAN

120 - Banff Avenue, Banff 762-3454

Greek & Eclectic. Sun-Sat, 11am - 11pm. Reservations accepted for 6 or more. Fully licensed. No non-smoking section. V, M, AE. Take-out. Moderate.

One of Banff's better eateries is the Balkan. It's also one of the prettier, a traditional Mediterranean blue and white place with planters and bright sunlight. The largeness of the room is broken up by various levels and quiet corners. You can be tucked away with another person for a cozy meal or you can party away with a large group. Occasionally during the winter months, a belly dancer heats up the room with her bangles and finger cymbals.

Their Greek food is a rich and real rendition. Garlic sways the hummus and tzatziki. The horiatiki (Greek salad) is redolent with feta and olives. And lemon slices through the calamari. The calamari at the Balkan are the breaded and fried variety, but they're still tender and fresh. Their lamb is likewise very good, either as an herbed and roasted leg or on a skewer as souvlaki. The souvlaki — whether lamb, chicken, beef, or pork — are among the most popular dishes. Served with potatoes, rice, and salad, it makes for a huge platter of food. No skimping here.

For years the Balkan has run the Banff Winter Carnival's Caesar salad competition. Although sometimes the event doesn't quite get off the ground, it's a potent one when it does. Over the years only a handful of winners has exceeded the quality of the Balkan's own rendition. It has as much flavour and as much romaine and croutons as a Caesar can stand.

If you think that Caesars are odd for a Greek restaurant, check out the rest of the menu. The lunch one offers very little Greek fare — only horiatiki, souvlaki, moussaka, and donairs. The rest of the menu is a '90s collection of diner fare — sandwiches, burgers, melts, omelettes, pastas, stir-fries, and salads. The dinner menu also has burgers and pastas and stuff, though it's made up predominantly of Greek offerings. It just goes to show that there's more than one way to get pleasantly Balkanized.

THE BISTRO

Wolf & Bear Street Mall, Banff 762-8900

Eclectic. Sun-Sat, noon - midnight. Reservations accepted.
Fully licensed. No non-smoking section. V, M, AE.
Moderate.

Finding a quiet place to eat in Banff is difficult, unless you live there. Finding a restaurant that's reasonably priced is almost as hard. Perhaps this obvious gap in the market is why The Bistro came along. Initially called the Theatre Bistro, they changed their name because too many customers assumed that live theatre was performed there.

At the corner of Wolf and Bear — that's a block behind the refurbished King Eddy — it sits in a new building that houses the town offices and the Lux cinemas. It's a north-facing space with lots of windows that don't look onto anything particularly interesting. With a wood and dark-green interior, it has captured a bistro feel while maintaining a mountain flavour. And though the food is far from cheap, you can eat there without taking out a second mortgage.

Menus in Banff look a little different than in Calgary. They're more international, probably due to all the tourists and European chefs. It seems like every second restaurant has carpaccio (thinly sliced raw beef), tiramisu (the super trendy Italian dessert), balsamic vinegar, and baguette. The Bistro goes worldwide with items like veal bratwurst, chicken curry, bouillabaisse, and tagliatelli Oriental (a noodle dish with seafood, snow peas, and leeks in teriyaki sauce). And for those going Canadian, there are beef dips, buffalo burgers, and marinated salmon.

Feeling nationalistic the day I lunched there, I tried the latter two dishes and both were just fine. The salmon, marinated gravlax-style with dill (actually a Scandinavian technique), was served on toast with a lovely mustard sauce. A good portion for $3.50. The buffalo burger was good too, but fell victim to a problem inherent with this meat: Buffalo is so low in fat that burgers can easily dry out before they're cooked all the way through.

My companion started with the house pâté encased in pastry. Not bad, though it could have used more seasonings. Then she ordered the spinach salad with mussels. They were unfortunately out of mussels that day, so they used artichoke hearts instead. The salad was big and packed with goodies for $4.75.

For dessert, there are seasonal berries, crème caramel, tiramisu, crêpes, and sundaes. California, British Columbia, France, Italy, Germany, and Spain are all represented on a reasonably priced wine list. And twenty-four of the wines are offered by the glass, something that I really like. So The Bistro is a pretty fair place to visit in Banff, especially with the pleasant staff.

BOCCALINO OF CANMORE

2, 1000 - 7 Avenue, Canmore 678-6424

Italian & Swiss. Tues-Sun, open 5pm for dinner (also open 5pm Mon for dinner in July & Aug). Reservations recommended. Beer, wine & liqueurs. No non-smoking section. V, M. Take-out. Moderate.

When the present husband-wife team took over the Boccalino in 1987, they faced one of the most difficult tasks in the world of restaurateurs. How do you follow the original owners who made the Boccalino such an extraordinary restaurant?

Before I get to the answer, I must admit to a problem that I personally have in reviewing this restaurant. I worked with the wife of this duo for three years in a non-restaurant business. It's difficult to review the efforts of people I know so well. Anyway, here goes.

The differences between the new and the old Boccalino are more subtle than obvious. Both chefs are young German-Swiss men with similar backgrounds. So the menu still features pastas, pizzas, and fondue. But the atmosphere and attitude of the place is just a little warmer now.

It's a tiny room that seats twenty-two people. They could probably cram another three or four chairs in, but they fortunately haven't. It's comfortable with its checkered tablecloths and tempting Swiss tourism posters.

A group of us dropped by to replenish our burnt calories after a day of hiking and found the perfect meals for our hunger. The Caesar salad balanced lemon, parmesan, and garlic. A thick, homemade mushroom soup arrived steaming — seldom have I tasted better. The daily appetizer special of bünderfleish (air-dried beef made in Canmore by Valbella Meats) was plentiful at only $4.50, and the slices of fresh bread disappeared quickly.

Our entrées were equally excellent. The scaloppine all'limone, two slices of tender veal drenched in a lemon sauce, had the tangy bite of citrus blended with cream and a secret spice. It had to be the best lemon sauce I've ever tasted. One of our friends who is known for her hummingbird-like appetite wiped out a huge plate of spaghetti gamberetti (jumbo shrimp and tomatoes in a cream sauce). My fettuccine primavera diverged from the typical vegetable and pasta dish by focussing on bacon, spinach, and mushrooms in its rich, heavy tomato sauce. Delightful.

Not satisfied to settle for this huge meal (it was a five hour hike after all), we dove into dessert. A Cointreau cheesecake with chocolate shavings and kiwi proved to be wonderful. And my Boccalino berries were embarrassingly decadent: A huge sherbet glass filled with vanilla ice cream was topped with warm, wine-sauced raspberries, which in turn were topped with whipped cream. Hot, cold, frosty, winey, creamy — oh boy!

To go with all this, we ordered an excellent bottle of Barbera for only $12.50 — a stunning wine deal for a restaurant, especially after seeing Piat D'Or at Chateau Lake Louise for $21.50. Combine that with polished, friendly service, and you have a very fine restaurant. And we didn't seem to be treated differently than other patrons. My only suggestion would be to stretch the complexity of the menu in order to truly reveal the talents of the chef.

I think the current husband-wife team has really established their own personality in the place. They have met their challenge admirably and deserve their own recognition.

BUFFALO MOUNTAIN LODGE

Tunnel Mountain Road, Banff 762-2400

Contemporary. Sun-Sat, 7am - 11pm. Reservations preferred. Fully licensed. No non-smoking section. V, M, AE, ER. Hotel lounge. Summer outdoor dining. Moderate-expensive.

Pushed up Tunnel Mountain away from the madding crowds of Banff Avenue, Buffalo Mountain Lodge has the pristine image that so many alpine hotels strive for but don't achieve. Elk outside the dining room are common here, squirrels almost a nuisance. It's mountain elegance at its best.

Buffalo Mountain is not one of the turn-of-the-century classics. It's a relatively new resort with all the modern accoutrements, like insulation and computers. Highlighting the lobby is a huge chandelier made of interwoven elk antlers — it must be ten feet across. The dining room is dark green with natural wood and windows that sweep up the walls. Opaque lamps dangle over floral-patterned chairs and tartan-clad waitresses.

Lunch and dinner is very "up-mountain" with items like a fresh herb frittata, a buffalo-mozzarella and grape quesadilla, seafood sausages, and paprika pasta with smoked goose and sun-dried tomatoes in a ginger sauce. And the prices aren't too outrageous considering that we're talking about Banff. Pork tenderloin in a Calvados, cream, and fig sauce is $16. A marinated venison loin with oyster mushrooms in a grape and port sauce is $20. If you're looking for something simpler (and cheaper), the bacon burger is $7, and the chicken breast sandwich is $8. So you should be able to find something to fit your mood and your budget.

The menus show a real commitment to fresh, seasonal foods combined in exciting ways. Take breakfast for example. Although you can get the hearty mountain meals of steak and eggs or hotcakes with bacon, there's a smoked salmon, cream cheese, and dill omelette or French toast topped with blueberries and glazed apples. At the bottom of the menu is an eggs Benedict with smoked goose breast and raspberry hollandaise. You don't see that too often. Replacing the basic ham with goose is a stroke of genius that works wonderfully. And lots of raspberries are swirled into the hollandaise. But it's served in a small oblong tray, and the yolk tends to run over the edge onto the plate below. They could just put it on the plate to begin with. But what the heck — you don't have to wash those extra dishes.

Buffalo Mountain's breakfast breads and pastries are just fine too, but their habit of leaving jam pots on the table disturbs me. I'm not fond of my wife's toast crumbs in the strawberry jam, let alone some previous diner's. I'd rather have individual servings than communal pots.

One last thing. Buffalo Mountain has almost conquered the problem of turning Banff's water into coffee. It's certainly worth sipping while watching the sun rise and the squirrels frolic.

CHEZ FRANCOIS

Highway 1A (Green Gables Inn), Canmore   678-6111

French. Sun-Thurs, 4:30pm - 10pm; Fri & Sat, 4:30pm - 11pm; Sun-Sat, 7am - 2:30pm. Reservations recommended. Fully licensed. No non-smoking section. V, M, AE, ER. Lounge. Summer outdoor dining. Moderate-expensive.

Dining in Canmore is getting to be tough — there are so many good places to choose from these days. And now along comes Chez Francois with a new look at traditional French food.

Chez Francois is in the new Green Gables Inn on Highway 1A. It's really a hotel coffee shop cum dining room, a place where I'd expect watery eggs and overdone beef. But it's blessed with the talents of a Quebecois couple who have settled in Canmore after a decade in Edmonton. Jean-Francois brings a deft hand to the kitchen, Sylvie brings warmth to the dining room.

The menu provides the first indication that there is some skill here. Not just anyone would attempt salmon stuffed with a shrimp and scallop mousse under hollandaise or serve rack of lamb with a sweet basil sauce. But dispel any thoughts of a heavy or starchy rendition of French cuisine. Although Jean-Francois' emphasis is on the classical, his food is fairly light.

The duck braised with Grand Marnier is a perfect version of duck à l'orange. Everyone's experienced the horrible old recipe that combines orange juice concentrate with cornstarch to make a rubberized lacquer for the poultry. Jean-Francois' rendition is nothing like that. The orange flavours ooze out of his thin sauce, brightening the juicy duck with citrus gusto. It tastes better with each bite. The seafood stew bathes an ocean of seafood in a smooth Pernod-touched sauce. A creamy three-peppercorn sauce coats tender filets of beef with a real bite. The filet of veal in wild mushroom sauce is good too, although the sauce could be pushed further. It's definitely headed in the right direction, but I would enjoy more wildness in the mushrooms.

The highlight of my meal here was a lobster bisque — rusty-orange coloured, spiked with brandy and tarragon, and topped with a dollop of fresh cream. The bowl had been set under a broiler to brown the cream, a presentation I had only seen in classical cookbooks, one I had never before sampled. It was superb, especially with the fresh baguette and a glass of crisp white wine. A few bowls of this and I would die happy. The cream of wild mushroom was full of flavour too. The nice thing about these soups was that they weren't too thick.

Between courses we were treated to a grapefruit and tequila granita to cleanse our palates. And for dessert we were tempted by an Alsatian apple pie made with custard, a frozen raspberry and chocolate mousse, a mandarin cheesecake, and specialty coffees. All decadent.

Throughout our evening, we received well-paced, professional service with a view of the Three Sisters at sunset. The room itself is a trendy blend of pinks and creams, all linened and lightened by wrap-around windows. Chez Francois is a pleasant surprise, and the price isn't bad for this style of food. Our meal for two, with appetizers, entrées, desserts, and a bottle of wine, came to $62.

I apologize to my wife who didn't want me to tell anyone about Chez Francois. It's too good to keep secret.

COZY CORNER

223 - Banff Avenue (Banff Avenue Mall), Banff 762-5082

German Deli. May-Oct: Sun & holidays, 11am - 5pm; Mon-Sat, 9am - 9pm. Nov-Apr: Mon-Sat, 10am - 6pm. Reservations accepted. Beer & wine. Non-smoking section. No credit cards. Take-out. Cheap.

It's hard to believe that any place on Banff Avenue is a cozy corner. But the Cozy Corner Deli & Eatery is. High-backed, carved pine booths provide privacy for a quick lunch. Largely Germanic food, there are sauerkraut soups, big sausages, creamy salads, and the best soup and sandwich deal in town at $5.25. You can eat in or take out or just pick up good quality supplies for your own riverside picnic. What else can I say about a place that carries a full line of Big Rock beer? Prost!

DES ALPES

702 - 10 Street, Canmore 678-6878

Swiss-French. Thurs-Tues, open 5pm for dinner. Reservations recommended, especially on weekends. Fully licensed. No non-smoking section. V, M. Moderate-expensive.

I've reviewed hundreds of restaurants on CBC Radio over the past decade. Every week at the end of my broadcast, I rate the eatery-of-the-week on a scale of 1 to 10. Until recently I had rated only two as high as 9.5. One was the Num-Ti-Jah Lodge on the Banff-Jasper highway in the mid '80s. The other was the original Boccalino in Canmore. The Boccalino is still a very fine restaurant, but it has changed hands. The talents and skills of Marianne and Xaver Schurtenberger, the Swiss couple who first owned it, are unique. To our good fortune, the Schurtenbergers built a new restaurant that opened in the fall of 1989.

They've put a lot of effort into Des Alpes, a two-storey chalet nestled in the evergreens by Policeman's Creek. The downstairs seats about forty-five in three distinct areas, and the family lives upstairs in typical Swiss fashion. Des Alpes is more upscale than its predecessor. Yet its oak and etched-glass interior, muted lighting, and bay windows exude an atmosphere where you'll be comfortable in jeans or a suit. The fireplace in one corner is balanced by a big display case stuffed with pastries and chocolates on the other side.

The question for me when Des Alpes opened was whether, after two and a half years, it would be as good as the old Boccalino. Would they have changed? Would my tastes have changed? Would the move to lighter cuisines be in opposition to the fullness of their Swiss-international style? I'm happy to report that they're not only as good as ever, they're even better.

It's the baking that really sells Des Alpes for me. The house bread is a light Swiss rye that can become a meal in itself if you're not careful. The cakes (my favourite being the chocolate-banana-rum with thick layers of chocolate and banana cream topped with more chocolate) taste better than they look. The fruit tarts, the cookies, the chocolates are all excellent. There is not a bakery in Calgary that produces this quality.

But don't go for just bread and dessert. Start with the Caesar salad, an old favourite from their Boccalino days. Not the least bit like the garlic-riddled Caesars which proliferate menus everywhere, this one is subtle and rich and creamy. Filled with herbs and topped with parmesan, it has an amazing dressing. If you want a more substantial appetizer, order the scallops meunière in butter, shallots, wine, and green peppercorns or a plate of European-style meats like air-dried beef and Black Forest ham.

Des Alpes' beef tenderloin in black peppercorn sauce is worth the drive from Calgary. Peppercorns float in a sauce that shines like patent leather shoes. A shine like this doesn't come from cornstarch. It comes from years of training and impressive skill. With a big swirl of linguine and vegetables of green beans wrapped in bacon and a half tomato filled with peas, it makes a memorable meal.

Their chicken ragout is in another rich sauce, this one based with cider. It has a strong combination of flavours — grilled chicken, sweet cider, tart apples. All round, a stunning dish unless the chef hasn't added enough cider. The cheese fondue, served with bread, raw vegetables, and pickles, is the best you'll get this side of Switzerland. Other main courses include pork tenderloin in curry, lamb with mustard and herbs, and trout with Noilly Prat sauce.

The hardest thing about eating at Des Alpes is trying to be delicate and polite when you have an irrepressible urge to lick your plate. Service is professional, the surroundings comfortable, the view great, the smells astounding, and the prices not bad. With appetizers, main courses, desserts, and a bottle of Australian Chardonnay, two can spend under $70. Of course you can spend a lot more than that too.

For me, Des Alpes is about as good as it gets. I can only take off points for two things. The butter is initially too cold and then too soft as it reaches room temperature (because it has been whipped). The whipped cream is dispensed from one of those spritzers, making it too airy. Subtracting .1 for each, that leaves Des Alpes with a score of 9.8 out of 10.

GALLAGHER HOUSE

637 - 8 Street, Canmore 678-5370

Eclectic & Afternoon Tea. Tues-Sun, 11:30am - 9pm. Reservations accepted. Beer, wine & liqueurs. No non-smoking section. V, M, AE. Summer outdoor dining. Moderate.

Most people's first impression of Gallagher House is that it's a wonderfully renovated old home. They're usually surprised to find that it was just built in 1986. It's a gorgeous grey and white Victorian mansion with a restaurant on the main floor and living quarters upstairs. You can feel elegant in a hand-knit nordic sweater here, yet the fine linens and crystal ensure you that no one is going to park their hiking boots on your lap. It epitomizes the class, charm, and comfort of Canmore. The main dining room is split by a fireplace, creating two cosy areas for enjoying an afternoon tea or an après cross-country feast.

The dinner menu suits the atmosphere with appetizers like pâté and baked brie, entrées like curried chicken, canneloni, and stuffed rainbow trout, and serious desserts like chocolate-rum pecan pie and carrot cake. Lunchtime is simpler with seafood melts, chicken pot pies, tourtières, and frittatas. All those luscious desserts are offered at tea time too (2:30 p.m. to 4:30 p.m.), as well as scones and teeny cucumber sandwiches.

We tried a good Caesar salad and a carrot-orange soup — a hot, pulpy version that could have leaned heavier on the orange. A great idea though and still tasty. I followed the soup with the "chicken artichoke," not a frightened vegetable but a huge boneless breast of chicken in a creamy white wine and artichoke sauce. The meat was tender, the sauce delicate — a perfect match. With a pile of saffron rice, some pea pods, and a baked tomato, it was a super dinner. The daily special of chicken Napoleon in a peach brandy sauce was likewise good, but could have been peachier. More fruit in the kitchen please.

An endless supply of hot rolls pleasantly melted us into the corner and prevented us from dealing with dessert — momentarily. Then we shared the lightest looking item on the menu, the frozen lemon soufflé. Tart lemon melded with whipped cream — very nice. I'll save the rest of those heavy-duty desserts for some chilly afternoon by the fireplace with a cup of tea. When the snow sifts down onto main street, there are few places I'd rather be.

JOE BTFSPLK'S

221 - Banff Avenue, Banff 762-5529

Diner & Bakery. Mon-Thur, 8am - 9pm; Fri-Sun, 8am - 10pm (check for extended high season hours). Reservations not accepted. Fully licensed. Non-smoking section. V, M, AE. Take-out. Cheap-moderate.

Remember the hard luck character with the unpronounceable name and the cloud over his head from the *L'il Abner* comic strip? Well, he's living on main street Banff these days, and his luck seems better most of the time.

Joe Btfsplk's is a diner with a strongly stylized '50s appearance in both food and decor. Shiny cherry-red vinyl covers chairs and booths, starkly offset by the black and white linoleum floor. It's a long, thin room with individual juke box selectors in the booths, a few tables, and a long lunch counter. Everything sparkled when it first opened, including the staff. But after a few years of serious Banff crowds, the vinyl is cracking and the white tile is scuffed. The staff don't seem as well-trained and proficient these days either. Although some have kept smiling and churning out ultra-service, others are sleepwalking through their work.

The food continues to be pretty good, though breakfast is only available until 4:30 p.m. What's a good diner without an all-day-all-night breakfast? But the clubhouse is still four inches thick, and the muffins still arrive steaming hot. So does the coffee, in plentiful quantities. The breakfast blue plate of two eggs; ham, bacon, or sausages; hash browns; and toast or a biscuit (before 4:30 remember) remains one of the better deals in Banff at $5.95. Those biscuits can easily withstand a serious mountain hike. The counter at the front features baking like cinnamon buns, Rice Krispie squares, Nanaimo bars, and butter tarts. Some are indifferent, but others are very good.

You'll always get a good bellyful at Joe's. Remember, Joe Bi-tif-spliks. For the hungry mountaineer.

JOSHUA'S

204 - Caribou Street, Banff 762-2833

Contemporary & Continental. Sun-Sat, 11:30am - 2pm, 5:30pm - 10:30pm. Reservations recommended. Fully licensed. No non-smoking section. V, M, AE. Pub. Moderate-expensive.

One of the hottest places to eat in Banff right now, a place where the locals go, is Joshua's. Only a few years ago Joshua's was a place to avoid, but it's gone through a great transformation recently with a new owner and a new chef and a new outlook on food.

It's still on Caribou Street, behind and across the street from the King Edward Hotel. It's small and inobtrusive, a ground level restaurant that seats fifty in the dining room and another thirty-five in the pub. The decor is a pleasant cross between northern California and southern Switzerland with wood, plants, heavy furniture, and clocks. One side of the restaurant is given over to the kitchen, which is fully open to view. You can watch your meal, and everyone else's, being prepared. There are two raised sections that create reasonably private areas, and it's one of the few restaurants in Banff where the tables aren't crunched together. Banff hasn't a smoking bylaw yet, so there is no distinct delineation for smokers, but they do try to accommodate their customers' wishes.

The menu is a creative Continental collection. Lunch changes monthly to reflect the season — in the summer you can order things like melon soup and fresh salmon with mint cream sauce. The dinner menu offers main courses of red meats, poultry, and seafood in various sauces, a daily fresh fish special, and a vegetarian entrée. Appetizers include smoked duck, chicken kabobs in a raspberry-ginger sauce, baked brie with mustard sauce, and a few soups and salads.

At a recent lunch I had what they call their six-onion soup made from white onions, shallots, garlic, green onions, leeks, and chives. It was much less forceful and pungent than I expected. Instead, it came out with a mild, delicate blend of onion flavours. A very nice way to start lunch. For my main course, I gave the daily special a try — fettuccine in cream sauce accompanied by chicken breast in a tomato coulis. The chicken and tomato were excellent. The coulis had been reduced to a perfect texture. The pasta was fresh and homemade, but the cream sauce didn't quite make the grade. Although aiming at a subtle, delicate flavour, I think the chef undershot a bit. Not that I expect my mouth to explode from a cream sauce, but this one lacked oomph. Even so, my meal fell within the understated style prepared at Joshua's — lightly spiced, quickly cooked, natural flavours.

Service is pretty good too. Sometimes it's rather perfunctory in Banff, but Joshua's seems to have a better handle on it than most places.

KANANASKIS COUNTRY GOLF COURSE

Highway 40, 31 Km S. of Trans-Canada 591-7070

Casual Eclectic. May-Oct: Sun-Sat, 6am - 10pm (hours vary seasonally). Reservations not accepted. Fully licensed. No non-smoking section. V, M, AE. Lounge. Summer outdoor dining. Cheap-moderate.

Kananaskis Country is an incredibly beautiful and, so far, tastefully developed piece of Alberta. The hiking and biking trails, the fishing, the sightseeing, the nordic and alpine skiing, and the golfing are all fantastic. When combined with fresh mountain air, they're also very appetite building. But I'm not impressed with the restaurants in Kananaskis Village. The best place to eat out here, though it's only open during our non-snow times, is still the golf course clubhouse.

This large wood, Alberta Tourism-style building overlooks the silica sand traps and the Kananaskis River as it flows through the two golf courses. There is an imposing feel of opulence as one gazes at the landscape, of well-spent Heritage dollars that probably irks a few people but satisfies many more. The building itself blends in, dwarfed by the natural beauty of its surroundings.

The dining room is progressively conservative — oops, I mean relatively conservative. Without the panorama it would pass as a highbrow truck stop. Only the carpet laid for spiked shoes is indicative of golf. Including the lounge, which constantly seems to be full of tall-tale telling golfers, there are about 120 seats indoors and another 80 outdoors — all serving a full food and beverage menu.

They serve what the public wants — an above average selection of salads, soups, sandwiches, and burgers along with steaks and fish and chips. Good, solid Alberta food. And it's prepared well. The salads are huge, loaded down with high-quality ingredients, the soups are hot and hearty. I always enjoy the burgers and the clubhouse sandwich no matter how many golf balls I've lost. I usually enjoy the service too. The only big disappointment is that, as of September 1990, they still do not carry Big Rock beer. Too inconvenient to sort the bottles they say. For my tax money, I'd like to see tourists sipping a good local beer rather than a Coors or a Bud.

In all though, it's a pleasant place for a good meal. A lot of people pass through in the summer, but the lineup for a seat moves fairly fast. And I understand that in the winter, the staff moves over to Nakiska to run the food services there.

LONE STAR CAFÉ

8 Street & 8 Avenue, Canmore 678-4901

Diner. Mon-Fri, 7am - 6pm; Sat & Sun, 8am - 7pm. Reservations not accepted. Unlicensed. No non-smoking section. No credit cards. Cheap.

With a 9 a.m. tee time at the Banff Springs, I arrived at the Lone Star by 7:45. Sure, I could have waited to indulge in an over-priced breakfast at the Springs itself, but why miss an opportunity to brush elbows with the ball-capped early risers at the Lone Star.

Small groups of men were leaning over construction blueprints and the *Sun*. A copy of the *National Enquirer* tattling on Oprah, Vanna, and Fergie decorated my pine slab table. A guy in suspenders reached into the self-serve coffee nook to pass the pot around. One more for the road.

At 7:55 my bratwurst and eggs were on the table. For $5.25 I also got hash browns and buttermilk pancakes. By 8:10 I was on my way with a freshly baked bran muffin tucked in my golf bag. (I considered a return visit for one of their great burgers or their hot chicken fingers later.) At 8:45 I was warming up on the first tee. The sun was shining, the three-iron felt good, and the Lone Star breakfast had smoothed out my drive. My first shot laid out two-hundred yards straight down the fairway. Maybe I'll start every round at the Lone Star.

MARTHA'S CAFÉ

730 - 9 Street, Canmore 678-2101

Eclectic. Sun-Sat, 8am - 9pm. Reservations accepted. Beer, wine & liqueurs. Non-smoking section. V, M, AE. Take-out. Moderate.

Martha's Café has been a big hit with the hiking boot crowd since it opened in 1987. And although I've never owned a pair of hiking boots, I like Martha's.

It's a converted house sporting natural wood and a homey feel. Windows open onto a beautiful view of the mountains. Fresh flowers often perk up the tables. The smell of baking fills the air. Martha's comes closer to capturing the essence of Canmore than any other restaurant in the area. The casualness is there — the open-air feel, the folksy flavour with a bit of polish. One foot is stuck in the '60s, the other is planted somewhere in the '90s. It feels a bit like a coffee-house — it's usually filled with a real healthy bunch, and there's a veggie burger on the menu. But there's also Black Forest ham and Dijon mustard on baguette and chromoly mountain bikes parked outside.

Breakfast is the best thing about Martha's, and you can order it until noon. It includes a choice between muesli or granola (if you can tell the difference), muffins, yogurt, French toast, and eggs scrambled with green onions, mushrooms, and cheddar cheese. Martha's buckwheat pancakes are the real thing. Almost black with buckwheat, they are thick and dense. The perfect pancake with the perfect bacon. With a small jug of maple syrup, they make the perfect breakfast.

The baking is usually impressive too. Martha's cinnamon buns, loaded with gooey cinnamon and walnuts or raisins, are among the best I've tasted. As with most baking though, they're best hot from the oven. But Martha's blueberry muffins are still amazingly good two days later. The chocolate-Grand Marnier cheesecake combines the ingredients into a lusciously smooth creation that tastes better than it looks. A standard carrot cake lacks the thud that I like, but is still good. The homemade brown bread is wholesome and available to purchase.

Martha's sandwiches would be great for a picnic. The smoked salmon with cream cheese and capers sounds like it would tempt the bears. There's also camembert with banana peppers, vegetables with pesto, and cucumber, cream cheese, and tomato. After 5:30 p.m. you can get fettuccine with prawns and red peppers, fettuccine with chicken breast and ginger, fettuccine with vegetables and soy sauce, and fettuccine Alfredo.

Martha's has a few other good things going for it. They brew great coffee. They also use local ceramic plates and cups and hang local art. All the staff have an infectious enthusiasm for the place and a clean scrubbed look. Just being around them makes me want to suck in my gut.

At press time I was told that Martha's would be changing owners. I was assured, however, that the menu and attitude would remain intact.

THE RED PEPPER

215 - Banff Avenue (Sundance Mall), Banff 762-4525

Thai & North American. Sun-Sat, 5pm - 10:30pm.
Reservations recommended. Fully licensed. No non-
smoking section. V, M, AE. Take-out. Moderate.

The owners of The Red Pepper are German-Swiss. The staff are French-Canadian, Australian, and Maltese. And they are serving Thai and North American food. A typical Banff mix.

Photos of the Thai royal family greet patrons, which is a good sign for a place cooking Thai. A few paintings that look like they came from a Thai garage sale and some Asian-looking pots decorate the room. Beyond that, it looks like it used to when it was a surf 'n' turf joint — lots of wood, greenish walls, a view of the parking lot.

Thai music flits through the air along with the aromas of curry, coriander, and chilies. The menu is filled with the multi-word Thai dishes. Things like thod man pla and nong gai piew wan. To assist in translation, they trundle over a photo scrapbook of each dish. That's very helpful.

It's not a huge Thai menu, but it's an adequate introduction to this style of food. There's a spicy shrimp soup with lemon grass and the omnipresent satays in peanut sauce. Bringing Thai to the Rockies are rainbow trout with basil leaves and salmon in chili paste.

I ordered two recommended dishes, the red curry pork and the chicken fried with basil leaves and chilies. These weren't actually recommended by the staff but rather by a vociferous young lady at a table across the room. She proclaimed loudly (and seemingly knowledgeably) that this was great food and that among her favourite dishes were the above-mentioned two. I figured that was as reasonable a recommendation as any.

The chicken is designated with the menu's three-star spiciness rating, plenty hot but not excessive. The poultry had been coarsely ground, an unusual way to serve it. But it worked very well, fried quickly without drying out. The pork in red curry, a two-star dish, was served in a clay pot over a little burner — I don't know why since it was hot enough as it was, and I gave it no chance to cool off. Anyway, the lean slices of pork were in a creamy, rich curry. A lovely dish. The waitress brought a pitcher of ice water to the table that I really didn't need (the food is spicy, but much hotter dishes exist elsewhere). A thoughtful touch though.

The Red Pepper is one of the more efficient places in Banff. Service is fast and friendly, the food skillfully and quickly prepared. Prices are perhaps a touch higher than comparable Thai places in Calgary.

There's also a short list of North American food ranging from burgers to blackened redfish that should keep non-Thai fans happy.

SILVER DRAGON

211 - Banff Avenue (Park Avenue Mall), Banff 762-3939

Cantonese & Peking. Sun-Sat, 11:30am - 11pm (open to midnight Fri & Sat in July-Sept). Reservations recommended. Fully licensed. No non-smoking section. V, M, AE, ER, JCB. Take-out. Moderate.

The first meal of dim sum I ever ate was at the Silver Dragon in Calgary's Chinatown about eighteen years ago. At that time it was a pretty exotic experience — trays of those delicate little snacks whistled by on carts steered by waiters in white jackets. I was impressed with the huge room decorated in red with lots of flashy gold figurines and Chinese symbols. And I enjoyed the food and service.

I was disappointed to discover that, although you can still have this Cantonese treat at the Silver Dragon in Calgary, it's not available at the newer Banff location. Nevertheless, the Silver Dragon is a reasonable addition to the mountain dining scene.

We tried the grilled pork and vegetable dumplings. They were tasty though not prepared with the greatest expertise. The dough wraps had been made about three times the size of the filling — every time we bit into one, it literally fell apart. Our chicken hot plate with black pepper sauce was pleasant but pretty tame compared to those available in other restaurants.

The Silver Dragon is a high-tech kind of place on the third floor of the Park Avenue Mall. The roof is one large skylight, so it's very bright for a Banff restaurant. Mirrors line the walls, and tables are set for five and six and eight, as well as two and four. The chairs are black bentwood, the tables are black and purple, and the waiters wear embroidered, double-breasted, padded-shouldered jackets. The Chinese plates are liberally laced with translucent beads, giving them an intriguing glow. Even the bathrooms are attractive with black tile and bizarre wallpaper.

The Silver Dragon has given Banff its first taste of ginger beef and chicken with cashews. And since its opening, it has increased the number of Peking dishes offered. It's comforting to know that, despite the lack of dim sum, Banff has a decent, well-run Chinese restaurant.

SUGINOYA

225 - Banff Avenue (Banff Avenue Mall), Banff 762-4773

Japanese. Sun-Sat, noon - 2pm, 5:30pm - 11pm (check for extended summer hours). Reservations recommended. Fully licensed. No non-smoking section. V, M, AE, JCB. Moderate.

There aren't too many places to escape the crowds of Banff Avenue and still stay on Banff Avenue. But the Suginoya is about as good as it gets. On the second floor of the Banff Avenue Mall, it's a perfect little island in a chaotic sea. With my shoes off, nestled into the *tatami* room cushions, I can feel totally dislocated — if they keep the FM rock radio turned down, that is.

The Suginoya is a fine Japanese oasis that has let Banff go to its head. The value is just not as high as it used to be. How could the assorted tempura have gone from $7.50 to $11, and the assorted sashimi from $10 to $16? Just because almost everyone else in Banff is pricy, it doesn't necessarily follow that they should be too.

But the food is still good. The gyu tataki of thinly sliced beef in ponzu sauce was tasty when I last had it. The beef was very rare, sort of a Japanese carpaccio. The sauce added a piquant, slightly sour flavour, enhanced by raw onions. A similar dish with deep-fried oysters is also good. Another tasty way to start your meal is with their dumplings or some miso soup.

The chicken teriyaki is served on a sizzling hot plate. Big pieces of tender chicken are grilled and served with vegetables and a bowl of rice, making a decent lunch or dinner. If you have a big appetite, order one of the multi-course combination meals. Or if you like to cook at your table, try the shabu shabu or the sukiyaki.

Although the food has maintained its quality, the staff has not. The last time I was there, I found them to be tired and snappish after a long tourist summer. And in spite of a fairly full restaurant and the presence of the sushi chef, they adhered to a policy of no sushi between 2 p.m. and 5:30 p.m. (During the summer, they are open throughout the afternoon.) So I am unable to confirm whether the Suginoya still has the best sushi in Banff. It sure looked good though.

But even with its faults, the Suginoya continues to be my choice for Japanese food in Banff.

BOW CORRIDOR

QUICK & EASY

THE BREAD BASKET BAKERY

628 - 8 Street, Canmore 678-4355

Mon-Sat, 8am - 6pm. No credit cards.

Pop's Bakery used to be one of my favourite points of interest in Banff, with great cake donuts, good cookies, and dense hiking breads. Then one day I parked my car out front before I noticed that it was gone. A new mega-mall was replacing it. I shed a tear.

A few months later someone in Canmore told me that he had bought bread at Pop's. Poor deluded soul I thought, until he explained that the Bread Basket in Canmore was the reincarnation of Pop's. So I drove down main street, parked right in front, and got my fix of oatmeal cookies and chocolate-coated cake donuts — just as good as before. Welcome back Pop.

THE CAKE COMPANY

220 - Bear Street, Banff 762-2330

Sun-Sat, 7:30am - 11pm. V, M.

It's pleasant to have a place to drop by for a cappuccino and a good piece of cake after a jog up Sulphur Mountain. Alas, they've stopped making my favourite, the lemon poppy seed cake — but there's still the raspberry buttercream cake and the dark-chocolate mousse cake, among others.

CASTLE CELLARS

302 - Caribou Street, Banff 762-3528

Mon-Sat, 11am - 11pm. V, M, AE, DC.

Banff's one and only private wine store, offering an alternative to the ALCB. Look for the entrance down some stairs just off Banff Avenue. (See wine entry in Calgary's Quick & Easy chapter.)

CHOCOLATERIE BERNARD CALLEBAUT

127 - Banff Avenue (Charles Reid Mall), Banff 762-4106

Mid May-mid Sept: Sun, noon - 9pm; Mon-Sat, 10am - 9pm. Mid Sept-mid May: Sun, noon - 6pm; Mon-Sat, 10am - 6pm. V, M, AE.

It's nice to have an alternative to all the overly sweet candies elsewhere on Banff Avenue. (See entry in Calgary's Quick & Easy chapter.)

DAMI'S GOURMET COFFEES & TEAS

722 - 8 Street (Kendall Mall), Canmore 678-2688

Mon-Sat, 10am - 6pm. V, M.

Can you think of another Alberta town the size of Canmore with its own coffee roasterie? You won't find one in Wetaskiwin or Oyen. The fact that Canmore has one shows the true alpine yuppie profile of this place — a great town with great taste.

Dami's took over Grewis Gourmet Coffees & Teas, but they have kept the same roasting processes. Dark, dark espresso, Noldy's rich blend, or Kenya AA can brighten the dreariest mountain morning. For those who like their caffeine in a different form, there's a selection of teas as well. And just in case you need a new pot, they carry all the coffee and tea accessories you could ever want.

JUST PIES CAFÉ

Bragg Creek Shopping Centre, Bragg Creek 949-3450

Tues-Sun, 10am - 6pm. No credit cards.

Just Pies Café has been packed since it opened its door in 1987 to make scads of quality pies, from a down-home apple to a knockout combo of black and blueberries called the Prize Fighter. The best partner to a piece of their pie is a cup of their house coffee, specially roasted at The Roasterie in Calgary. They also serve light lunches like soup or quiche in this totally non-smoking establishment.

VALBELLA MEATS

Elk Run Industrial Park, Canmore 678-4109

Mon-Fri, 8am - 5pm; Sat, 9am - 3pm. No credit cards.

Valbella Meats in Elk Run Industrial Park (east of the Trans-Canada on Highway 1A) is predominantly a meat processor that supplies restaurants, but they are open to the public as well. They make things like lamb sausage, smoked turkey, beef jerky, and mega-smoked pepperoni called chimney sticks — probably because they are pitch black. Perhaps the most unique product of the Banff-Canmore area is their bünderfleish (air-dried beef). Lean meat is mixed with herbs and spices and then cured in the fresh Rocky Mountain air for eight to twelve weeks. The texture and taste is equal to the best prosciutto.

VALBELLA'S DELI CORNER

215 - Banff Avenue (Sundance Mall), Banff 762-4819

Mon-Sat, 10am - 6pm. No credit cards.

If you can't make it to Valbella Meats in Canmore, their excellent products are available at Valbella's Deli Corner in Banff (even though the two places have different owners). Here you can also get your picnic fixings, from excellent in-house baked croissants and muffins to designer mustards and prepared salads. Homemade soups and sandwiches are available for knoshing out of styrofoam at one of their rough-hewn pine tables. This place is popular with Banffites, so watch out for lunchtime lineups.

THE FOOTHILLS

BLUE RIDGE

102 - Morrison Road, Longview 558-3930

Diner. Sun-Sat, 7am - 10pm. Reservations accepted. Fully licensed. No non-smoking section. V. Take-out. Cheap.

There aren't too many great country cafés left. Little places that act as the hub of the community while pouring gallons of coffee and baking heavy-duty pies. But the Blue Ridge in Longview is such a place. It sits next to the Esso station at the intersection of Highways 22 and 541. It's a non-descript square room washed with fluorescents. Kitchen tables sit on a worn carpet, and a massive collection of ball caps covers the walls — there must be hundreds of them.

The waitress arrived at our table a few seconds after us with menus, a coffeepot, and a dishrag to clear away the debris of our predecessors. The coffee and her smile warmed the room more than those ball caps.

I'm a sucker for dishes named after the restaurant I'm in. I guess I expect a certain amount of pride to be attached to the product. So, I ordered the Blue Ridge burger, a sturdy construction of three homemade patties, a slab of ham, processed cheese, and various standard accoutrements. It came with a bucket-load of fries and some onion rings. I had to laugh in amazement when it was delivered. Each pattie was about an inch thick, making this a burger I couldn't even get my hands around let alone my mouth. After maneuvering my plate for a minute, I looked up and spotted a regular who was about to eat the same thing. Before starting, he removed one of the patties altogether. He then leaned on the rest of the burger, squashing the whole thing down a couple of inches. So I did the same. Aside from its girth, the hamburger was fairly memorable for its taste. Not extraordinarily flavourful, but still a very fresh, old-style version. The clubhouse sandwich we ordered contained all the requisite ingredients piled high, with a huge side of fries. Both the raisin and the strawberry-rhubarb pies were good too, but made in the old-fashioned way with too much sugar.

The Blue Ridge menu is a masterpiece of diner food. Breakfasts of eggs, bacon, ham, sausage, toast, porridge, and hash browns. Then there are open Denvers, hot turkey sandwiches, crispy fried chicken, pork chops, lasagna, and oyster dinners. This is probably the only place in the world where a perogie platter with bacon, onions, and sour cream would be labelled as a light dinner.

The Blue Ridge provides a great stop for Kananaskis day-trippers as well as locals. From pre-schoolers to seniors, cowboys to hikers, everyone likes a side of fries and gravy once in a while.

BRIAR ROSE TEAROOM

153 - Macleod Trail, High River 652-3226

Light Lunch & Tea. Tues-Sun, 11am - 4pm (check for extended Christmas season hours). Reservations preferred, especially Sun. Unlicensed. Non-smoking section. V, M, AE, DC. Cheap-moderate.

Tromping through the Foothills on a weekend afternoon can really work up an appetite. Though there are a number of places to eat in High River, only one restaurant captures the historic elegance of that old ranching community. The Briar Rose Tearoom sits on the west edge of downtown in a house that was built about forty-five years ago by a retired ranching couple named Gillespie. I'm told that Mrs. Gillespie was an avid bridge player and that the house was designed to accommodate her large and frequent card parties in such a way that Mr. Gillespie could enter without disturbing the ladies.

The main floor, now reserved for the tearoom, is divided into three sunny rooms with a sizeable kitchen in the back. Upstairs is a gift shop with local and more far-reaching arts and crafts — you can practically smell the potpourri down the street. The whole place is very homey — like visiting a grandmother's house filled with cheerful voices and delicate aromas. And thoughtfully, two of the three dining rooms are reserved for non-smoking.

The Briar Rose puts all their eatable efforts into lunch and tea. High tea is one of the best deals going. A collection of savouries and little sandwiches, a tart, a piece of carrot cake, and of course, tea or coffee is quite reasonable with a price-tag of $6.

My mother likes tearooms. My father doesn't. He always complains when he gets dragged to another one that he doesn't get enough to eat. I think the folks at the Briar Rose realize that a lot of their clientele want more substantial meals too, so they've included hearty sandwiches like Monte Cristos, Reubens, and even peanut butter with banana. There's quiche and crêpes and stew, and for lighter appetites, there are lots of salads.

I take after my father so I ordered the chicken à la king served in puff pastry. It was filling and good, but could have used a bit more chicken.

My wife's croissant was loaded with cheddar, avocado, cucumber, alfalfa sprouts, and mushrooms. All very fresh, very tasty. Both meals came with fresh fruit to create a satisying lunch.

But of course, the real attraction of tearooms (besides the high teas) is the desserts. They told us that they have the best cheesecake in High River, but we both went for the banana cake, the recipe for which comes from Guyana. Although it was interesting, our pieces were a little light on banana and the delicious rum icing. But the way other customers were oohing and aahing over their cream puffs smothered in whipped cream and chocolate, it looks like they're satisfying a few sweet teeth.

Overall, I'd recommend the Briar Rose. It's not the quietest place for a cup of tea, but it's got a real friendly High River feel, and the food is pretty darned good.

CALGARY LOCATIONS

Centre St & 16 Ave N. Area

Amandine Bakery
Chili Club, The
Da Guido
Ercole
Hugo's Deli Cafe
La Pasta
Salt & Pepper
Santorini
Silver Inn
Trong-Khanh

Chinatown

Golden Fortune
Hang Fung
Hong Kong Bakery
Silver Dragon

Downtown

Beirut
Boulevard Cafe
Buzzards Café
Café Danois
Cedars, The
Claudio's Trattoria
Divino Cafe Gallery
Earl's
Fagin's
Green Street Café
Juan's
Kim's Donair & Jamaican Cuisine
La Paella
Little Bangkok
Market Square Grill (The Bay)
McQueens Upstairs
Original Phnom-Penh
Owl's Nest, The
Rimrock Room, The
Siam Sukiyaki
Simple Simon Pies
Sukiyaki House
Sushi Hiro
Yuzuki

4 St SW (10 Ave to Elbow River)

Earl's Tin Palace
Entre Nous
4 St. Rose
4 St. Rose General Store
Franzl's Gasthaus
Joey's Only
Salt & Pepper
Sam's Original Deli

Kensington Rd & 10 St NW Area

Bohemia Bistro
Café Ceres
Charly Chan's Rice House
Demetris Souvlaki
Diva Coffee Room
Gerard Chocolatier
Heartland Country Store
Island Experience - The Roti Shop
Kensington's Delicafé
Lori's Gourmet Delikatessen
Roasterie, The
Sam's Original Deli

Macleod Tr S. Area

Chocolate Bar, The
Dutch Pastry & Chocolaterie
Earl's
Home Food Inn
Joey's Only
Kam Han
La Piccola Napoli
Le Gourmet
Leo Fu's
Olive Grove
Phil's
Pies Plus
Rockin' Horse Saloon
Salt & Pepper
Taj Mahal

Northeast

Giovanni's
Husky House
Jenny's
Meelen Omar Khayyam
PizzaMaria

Northwest

Blue House Cafe
Cedars Falafel Hut, The
Chocolaterie Bernard Callebaut
Dairy Lane Milk Bar
Dutch Pastry & Chocolaterie
Earl's
Joey's Only
Naturbahn Tea House
Phil's
Shan Tung
Trattoria D'Italia

17 Ave S. Area (Crowchild Trail to Stampede Grounds)

Blue Vinny Deli-Cafe
Buon Giorno
Caffe Beano
Chianti
Chocolate Bar, The
Chocolaterie Bernard Callebaut
Cilantro
Decadent Desserts
Fiore Cantina
Gourmet Royal
Joey's Only
La Chaumière
La Ruelle
Lion's Den
Mont Blanc Pastry Shop
Moti Mahal
Peppers Deli
Phil's
Soup Kitchen, The
Stepps
Sultan's Tent
Tandoor
Wine Shop, The
Yervand's

Southeast

Amadeus
Big Rock Brewery
Blackfoot Truck Stop
Calgary's Farmers'
    Own Farmers' Market
Deane House, The
Dragon Pearl
Duck Worth Farm
Earl's
Henri's Galley
Jump-Start Café
Kam Han
Lake Sylvan Palace
Lloyd's Caribbean Bakery
Mimo
My Favorite Ice Cream Shoppe
Ogden Bake Shop
Phil's
Portugal Bakery
Saigon
Sausage King
Simple Simon Pies
Starlite

Southwest

Amandine Bakery
Bali
Bayou, The
Chocolaterie Bernard Callebaut
Dock, The
Dragon Pearl
Dutch Pastry & Chocolaterie
Gallo's
Glamorgan Bakery
J. Webb Wine Merchant
King & I, The
Le Flamboyant
Leo Fu Take Out
My Favorite Ice Cream Shoppe
Pegasus
Piazza Steak House
Sizzling Wok, The
Sparky's Diner
Spiros Pizza
You're So Sweet Noodle House

This index includes some reliable places that are not reviewed in this book.

INDEX

NOTES

John Gilchrist reviews restaurants for CBC Radio's Calgary Eye Opener every Friday morning at 7:50 a.m. He also writes the Gastronomy column for *CinemaScope* magazine. His 1987 edition of *My Favourite Restaurants* was a National Best Seller and received a special mention from the 1987 Alberta Non-Fiction Awards.